ON BECOMING
A SCHOOL LEADER

A Person-Centered Challenge

ARTHUR W. COMBS

ANN B. MISER

KATHRYN S. WHITAKER

Association for Supervision and Curriculum Development
Alexandria, Virginia USA

ASCD™

Association for Supervision and Curriculum Development
1703 N. Beauregard St. • Alexandria, VA 22311-1714 USA
Telephone: 1-800-933-2723 or 703-578-9600 • Fax: 703-575-5400
Web site: http://www.ascd.org • E-mail: member@ascd.org

Gene R. Carter, *Executive Director*
Michelle Terry, *Associate Executive Director, Program Development*
Nancy Modrak, *Director, Publishing*
John O'Neil, *Acquisitions Director*
Julie Houtz, *Managing Editor of Books*
Carolyn R. Pool, *Associate Editor*
René Bahrenfuss, *Copy Editor*
Robert Land, *Proofreader, Indexer*

Charles D. Halverson, *Project Assistant*
Gary Bloom, *Director, Design and Production Services*
Karen Monaco, *Senior Designer*
Tracey A. Smith, *Production Manager*
Dina Murray, *Production Coordinator*
John Franklin, *Production Coordinator*
Cynthia Stock, *Desktop Publisher*

Printed in the United States of America.

February 1999 member book (p). ASCD Premium, Comprehensive, and Regular members periodically receive ASCD books as part of their membership benefits. No. FY99-5.

ASCD Stock No. 199024
ASCD member price: $18.95; nonmember price: $22.95

Library of Congress Cataloging-in-Publication Data

Combs, Arthur W. (Arthur Wright), 1912–
    On becoming a school leader : a person-centered challenge /
Arthur W. Combs, Ann B. Miser, Kathryn S. Whitaker.
    p. cm.
    Includes bibliographical references and index.

    ISBN 0-87120-336-7 (pbk.)
    1. Educational leadership. 2. School management and organization.
I. Miser, Ann B., 1943– II. Whitaker, Kathryn S. III. Title.
    LB2806 .C649 1999
    371.2—ddc21   98-58054
                                                   CIP

04 03 02 01 00 99   10 9 8 7 6 5 4 3 2 1

ON BECOMING A SCHOOL LEADER
A PERSON-CENTERED CHALLENGE

INTRODUCTION

OVER THE PAST 50 YEARS, THE WORLD HAS SEEN A DRAMATIC
shift in knowledge about human nature and how people learn and
change. Many psychologists have moved from things-oriented, behaviorist concepts to views that are more person centered. Yet not
everyone has taken advantage of the best of this modern thinking.

Education reform faces a crippling gap between the person-
centered approach and many educators' current practice. The dis-
crepancy is particularly critical for educational leaders. Their work
heavily depends on relationships with people—such as faculty and
staff members, students, other administrators, and parents—and on
community and public expectations. *On Becoming a School Leader:
A Person-Centered Challenge* explores the significance of person-
centered thinking for leadership in education.

About This Book

Section I of this book describes why it is important for school
leaders to understand how people's belief systems drive their personal
and professional behavior. Section II focuses on the need for school
leaders to understand how and why people respond to, or resist,

change. Section III focuses on how organizations influence person-centered leadership and how leaders, in turn, influence organizations.

More specifically, Chapter 1 introduces the concept of person-centered, as opposed to things-centered, leadership. It reinforces the idea that school leaders must understand the types of behavior that facilitate and encourage high performance among staff members and students.

Chapter 2 describes the kinds of data that leaders should seek and use in the innumerable tasks of their daily work. It shares examples of how successful school leaders avoid potential problems by purposely pursuing specific kinds of information. These leaders understand that a person's behavior should not be viewed in isolation, free of an interpretive context. Instead, behavior offers a way to discern the internal meanings a person has given to a situation.

Chapter 3 provides a foundation for understanding human motivation for behavior and action. This includes the concepts of threat and challenge. The chapter also touches on why it is important for school leaders to have healthy self-concepts.

Chapter 4 centers on the need for school leaders to develop a climate where learning and change can flourish. This chapter describes the heart of a learning organization. It also describes how a school that focuses on learning and change can benefit teachers and other adults, as well as students.

Chapter 5 more fully illustrates the importance of a healthy self-concept for school leaders, reinforcing several of the psychological principles discussed in Chapter 3. Before leaders can facilitate healthy self-concepts in others, they first must look at their own needs and behaviors to see if they are developing a thriving person within. Organizations frequently mirror their leaders' self-concepts; therefore, it is crucial for school leaders to have balanced and sound personal belief systems that guide their daily behavior.

Chapter 6 portrays several examples of how person-centered leaders help develop positive self-concepts in others. It explores how schools are affected when leaders take the time to encourage, inspire, and advocate the positive development of all individuals. This is a daunting, but crucial, task.

Chapter 7 focuses on why a person-centered leader must demonstrate purpose and commitment. Purpose is characterized through policies, procedures, and daily events. This chapter also reinforces the need for clarity of purpose in all that a leader does. Further, Chapter 8 illustrates the vital role of authenticity in developing a healthy organization. This chapter considers the authenticity of the leader's behavior and authenticity in the systems the leader develops. Such authenticity allows for open, honest dialogue where people are not afraid to share their true thoughts and emotions.

Chapter 9 portrays the symbiotic relationship between leaders and organizations. It suggests that all parts of the organization are so closely intertwined that whatever happens at one level must necessarily affect the rest of the organization. Leaders are accustomed to controlling an organization's events through goals and activities, but organizations have a life within that must be acknowledged and honored. This life has nothing to do with external controls that leaders may attempt to impose.

Finally, Chapter 10 discusses needed changes for university preparation programs. It offers specific suggestions for changes that will foster a more person-centered approach to the preparation of future school leaders.

About Our Experiences

The writing team for this book brings together the thinking and experience of a person-centered psychologist/educator and two educational leaders, each with long and successful careers as teachers, principals, innovators, and trainers of educational leaders. As a result of our collaboration on this book, we have a new empathy and respect for the complex, demanding occupation of school administration. We also have come to see the work of educational leaders from a new and challenging perspective. We have tackled old problems from new directions, and we have explored and discovered innovative ways of being and becoming as people and as professional educational leaders.

We feel richly rewarded by this experience and hope our attempt to convey these explorations to others will be equally challenging and helpful. The new understanding about people and their relationships has important implications for almost every aspect of educational leadership. These kinds of understanding have the potential to improve the education process for all students and to foster each educational leader's personal and professional success and satisfaction.

LEADERSHIP AND BELIEF SYSTEMS

A Person-Centered Perspective on Educational Leadership

Every day, educational leaders confront problems with both things *and* people. Few leaders fail because they are unable to cope with things. When leaders blunder, it usually is because they have dealt ineffectively with people. A major reason for such difficulties is that leaders have not changed their basic assumptions about human behavior. They continue to deal with people using age-old methods that worked well with things.

The Industrial Model

For thousands of years, we humans have faced the never-ending task of taming things and making them serve our needs for food, clothing, and shelter. To that end, we attempted to control and manipulate all aspects of our environment. It was natural, then, to

---

Authors' note: All names of people in examples and scenarios in this book are pseudonyms, except where indicated.

apply methods that worked well with material things to work with people. We call this the "manipulation-of-forces" approach.

Even as cultures became more complex, leaders still applied the same techniques to managing people. Later, with the development of psychology, the manipulation-of-forces approach gained "scientific" confirmation through behaviorist, or stimulus-response, psychology. These theories contend that people behave as a consequence of the stimuli they confront. The way to change behavior, therefore, is to manipulate the forces exerted on people.

That conception of how to deal with people is still widespread throughout the things-oriented, technological society of the United States. Given the ages-long experience of the culture—and corroboration through the science of psychology—it is not surprising that so many educational leaders use the manipulation-of-forces concept for working with people in schools. Most books on leadership, for example, deal primarily with the following:

- what leaders ought to do or think about education and their jobs,
- what they ought to do about the problems they face, and
- the professional characteristics they should possess.

Training programs generally mirror those assumptions, which results in curriculums that concentrate on "things" such as school management, school law, administrative theory, financial planning, and school organization.

This preoccupation with things has been influenced deeply by educational leaders' penchant for looking to industry for models of desirable ways to think, act, and organize schools. This makes some sense, since industry is intent on the production of things and schools must deal with certain "things." However, such industrial models are inappropriate for the person-centered aspects of leadership. Industrial workers are regarded as part of the machinery to bring about the production of things. In education, students are the product, and the goal of teaching is student welfare. If industry were designed for the welfare of its workers, it surely would not be organized the way it is.

Changing Beliefs About People

What we believe about the nature of human beings and how they behave has implications in all aspects of our lives. These beliefs provide the basic assumptions from which we decide how to cope with people, whatever the setting. Our beliefs about people also affect the ways we regard ourselves and those with whom we interact. They determine how we raise our children and treat our husbands, wives, or parents. They influence the structure of our institutions and what we expect of government. In the school setting, these beliefs affect how teachers teach and leaders lead. It is vitally important, then, that leaders act from the most accurate concepts about human behavior.

A major problem for educational reform is the gap between current practice and the best modern thinking about what people are like and how they learn. About 50 years ago, psychology began to conceptualize a different way of understanding people, learning, and change. This approach to behavior is called by a number of names: humanist, existential, cognitive, perceptual, or person-centered psychology. Whenever ideas change about what people are like and why they behave as they do, the implications extend into every aspect of culture. That is happening now with the shift to person-centered understandings.

Person-centered thinking is especially important for education. Unfortunately, the new understandings are working their way into the mainstream of educational thought and practice very slowly. One reason for this lag between the best we know and its implementation in schools is the fact that most educational leaders are unaware of the person-centered movement or are not trained in its requirements (Combs & Gonzalez, 1997).

The person-centered view of people contends that we do not respond directly to the forces exerted on us. Instead, we behave in terms of the meanings or perceptions that exist for us at the moment we act. More specifically, people behave according to how they see themselves, the situations they confront, and the purposes they seek to fulfill. Offering someone two tickets to the opera, for example, will prompt quite different responses depending on the meaning the tickets have for the person to whom they are offered. An opera buff will accept them with thanks. A friend who does not care for opera but is embarrassed to refuse your generous gift may accept the tickets and give them to someone else. An acquaintance in need of cash may accept the tickets just to sell them to someone else.

The idea that people behave in terms of the forces exerted on them is only partly right—and few things are as dangerous as a partly right idea. It's true that people *sometimes* seem to behave as a result of forces exerted on them. This accounts for why many leaders continue to apply the manipulation-of-forces concept: Partly right ideas *sometimes* get results. Leaders who use the manipulation-of-forces method hope that if they try even harder, with greater care and discipline, surely the method will work the way they want every time. It doesn't. It is time to recognize that the manipulation-of-forces concept for dealing with people is only partly right. Now is the time to embrace a new, more appropriate understanding.

The Person-Centered Perspective

Aside from the family, education is the most person-centered of all institutions. And to fulfill their roles in education effectively, teachers and other school leaders must understand the fundamental assumptions of person-centered thinking. They need to develop a new conception of educational leadership from a person-centered orientation.

It has long been assumed that effective teaching, counseling, or leading primarily is a matter of knowledge about content, methods, and practice. As a matter of fact, recent research into the difference between good and poor practitioners in a number of helping professions, including education, is unable to make such discriminations on the basis of either knowledge or methods (Combs & Avila, 1985). Knowledge of subject matter is no guarantee of effectiveness on the job. Almost everyone can attest to this fact from personal experience with teachers who knew the subject but could not teach "worth a darn."

The evidence for methods is no better. A review of hundreds of research studies seeking to discover the methods of effective practitioners leads to the conclusion that there is no such thing as a "good" or "right" method that can be clearly associated with either good or bad performance (Combs, 1982). The observation is true for educational leaders as well. If effective educational leadership is not a question of knowledge or methods, what does make the difference?

To find that answer, we must begin from the understanding that people behave according to how things seem to them. More specifically, people behave according to how they see themselves, how they see the situations they confront, and the purposes they hold at the moment in which they act. That principle applies to leaders, just like anyone else.

Leaders behave in terms of their beliefs—thousands of beliefs. They especially hold beliefs about themselves, the people and situations they work with, and the purposes they seek to fulfill. In light of that understanding, an educational leader's growth must be seen as a lifelong task of personal being and becoming. It is a matter of developing beliefs about self, the people and tasks confronted, and the goals the leader wants to achieve.

Modern brain research tells us that the human brain is a magnificent organ whose primary function is to make meaning of experience. Leaders, like everyone else, continuously explore, revise, adapt, and construct a personal belief system to act as a map or as guidelines for action. Think of a belief system as a personal theory for determining behavior. The most trustworthy belief systems will be accurate, comprehensive, simple, internally consistent, and stable (though open to appropriate change). Acquiring and refining such a belief system is a lifelong project.

This person-centered view of human personality and behavior has ramifications for every aspect of leadership, whether it be the selection of candidates, leadership preparation programs, continued growth of people on the job, relationships with faculties and the public, the design and function of programs, or the leader's own personal and professional satisfactions. Whenever our ideas about human behavior change, they open the door to new ways of dealing with old problems and generate the excitement and promise of innovation and new achievement. The person-centered concept generates a new perspective on leadership, offers new ways of looking at some of education's knottiest problems, and opens promising new fields for research.

Two Tools for Leaders

Educational leaders still must deal with "things." They have to handle budgets, equipment, supplies, and physical facilities. For those kinds of problems, the manipulation-of-forces concept still provides a useful guideline for action. However, leaders now have a second option for dealing with the human aspects of leadership. They can apply person-centered thinking to the human aspects of education. In any occupation, workers with two tools for their tasks have an advantage over people with only one. A successful leader understands both the manipulation-of-forces view and the person-centered approach—and when to use each appropriately.

Traditional leadership approaches generally concentrate on the leader's behavior. Behaviorist psychology corroborated that frame of reference and suggested that the causes of behavior lay in the forces exerted on people. Humanist, perceptual-experiential views now postulate that the causes of behavior lie in a person's perceptions or belief systems. Thus, from a person-centered perspective, educational leadership must be understood in terms of the belief systems of leaders and the belief systems of those they want to lead. Leaders who seek self-improvement will need to spend less time on the search for "right" methods and more on the exploration and refinement of their belief systems.

Good and Poor Practitioners

A series of research studies on the difference between good and poor practitioners in six professions reveals that good performers can be discriminated clearly from poor ones on the basis of the beliefs they hold in at least five areas:

1. data being sought and responded to,
2. what the leader believes about people,
3. what the leader believes about self,
4. the leader's purposes, and
5. the leader's authenticity (Combs & Soper, 1963).

Before examining each of these critical areas more closely, it is important to recognize that having an idea does not necessarily make it a vital factor in a person's professional practice. There is a vast difference between knowing and behaving. The effectiveness of a belief depends on its strength or personal relevance.

Research on teachers' beliefs, for example, finds that both good and poor teachers do equally well on tests of what they "ought to" or "should" espouse. Few of us behave ineffectively because we do not know what we "ought" to do. When we misbehave, it is because we do not believe some principle deeply or strongly enough to act on it, or because some other belief seems to have greater relevance at the time we act.

The Leader's Data

We have seen that people do not behave according to the forces exerted on them. Instead, they behave in terms of their beliefs, meanings, or perceptions. Thus, the primary data with which leaders must work are the perceptions and beliefs of the people they want to lead. This fact is borne out in research on good and poor workers in a number of helping professions.

Good practitioners are always keenly aware of how things seem to those with whom they work. Poor practitioners, on the other hand, are preoccupied with how things seem to themselves. This was highlighted in a discussion between a sensitive supervisor and a teacher who asked for help with one of her students.

> "I don't know what to do with him," the teacher said. "I know he can do the work, but he won't even try! I tell him, 'It's easy, Jimmy. You can do it.'"
> At this point the supervisor broke in, "Jane, don't ever tell a child that something is easy." The supervisor then went on to explain, "If you tell a child a thing is easy, and he can't do it, the only conclusion he can come to is that he must be stupid. If you tell him it's easy, and he can do it, now look what you have done. There's no glory in doing something only to have folks tell you, 'Well, it was easy!'"
> She continued, "Tell him it's hard, Jane, but you think, pretty sure, he could do it. Then, if he can't do it, he hasn't lost face. And if he can do it, what a glory that is for him!"

When we understand how things look to the other person, it is more likely that our actions will be on the mark. Yet being aware of how others see things seems like an impossible task since people's perceptions are inside their minds and not open to direct examination. Actually, people tell us all the time how they are thinking and feeling. The question is whether we are properly receptive.

Because people behave in terms of their perceptions or beliefs, it is possible to "read behavior backward" and arrive at a fairly accurate grasp of what they think and feel. The process is called "inference," and we all have done it since early childhood. Children are notoriously sensitive to how the adults who surround them think and feel. The process of reading behavior backward also is known as "empathy," the capacity to put yourself in another person's shoes and to see things from that point of view. Good counselors, teachers, and leaders exhibit empathy all the time.

To read behavior backward, begin by careful observation of what a person does. Next, ask yourself, "How would a person have to perceive, feel, or believe to behave like that?" Often, the answers to that question are self-evident. For example, it does not take great genius to grasp what a mother is feeling or what she is concerned about as she cries, "My child is failing 1st grade! How can I face my friends?"

Less stressful circumstances may require longer periods of observation to decipher behavior. As you form hypotheses, you can then make further observations to check the accuracy of your inferences, modifying or confirming as needed. By reading behavior backward in this way, it often is possible to understand other people with such accuracy that you can predict how they are likely to behave in the future.

Empathy is an important skill for anyone who works with people. It provides essential data for all leaders. It also is a skill that doesn't have to be learned. We all learned to make such inferences in childhood, and we maintain the ability throughout life. We are all deeply sensitive, for example, to how husbands, wives, children, lovers, bosses, coworkers, friends, or enemies feel and think. In daily life, however, it is easy to restrict the use of empathy to those people who are important to us, and we neglect the skill with people we feel we can safely ignore. Acting empathetically is not a question of special training. It is simply doing what we already know how to do, only doing it consciously, carefully, and systematically, even with people we normally might overlook.

Being truly empathic requires personal discipline. It requires taking time to really listen to others, which is very difficult for some people. Empathy also requires being willing to set aside our own feelings and beliefs to understand someone else. This may call for self-control or suppression of our own needs. Our own ways of seeing things have such a feeling of being "right" and "obvious" that we think they must feel the same to others as well. It is easy to jump to the conclusion that if others don't see things as we do, they either must be stupid or perverse.

Though educational leaders work with both things and people, people are the most crucial to their efforts. A things-oriented culture values objectivity and logic, but people behave in terms of their beliefs, feelings, attitudes, values, hopes, fears, loves, hates, and aspirations. When dealing with people, logic is often only a systematic way of arriving at the wrong answer. It is vitally important for leaders to have an accurate conception of the causes of behavior so they can form trustworthy maps or guidelines for making decisions. People do not behave according to the facts, nor are people objective. They behave according to their personal meanings, perceptions, or beliefs. These qualities determine behavior, and they are the data with which person-centered leaders must work.

The Leader's Beliefs

What leaders believe about the people they work with is of major significance. This is borne out in research on good and poor practitioners in the helping professions (Combs & Avila, 1985). Good helpers believe the people they work with are able, dependable, worthy, and friendly. For example, it makes a great deal of difference whether a leader believes people are able. If you don't believe folks are able, then you don't dare let them be! If you do not believe they are able, you must take charge and make sure they get where they should go. Such a belief certainly will show in a leader's behavior.

Coworkers' responses will be very different toward leaders who feel people are able and those who have grave doubts about their employees' capacities. Who has not responded with energy and enthusiasm to a supervisor's words of praise or encouragement? And who has not felt self-doubt and humiliation from a real or imagined put-down by someone whose opinion was important?

Empathy is natural to everyone. We are all deeply sensitive to the feelings, attitudes, and beliefs of those around us, particularly if they have authority over us. So it is that a leaders' beliefs about people affect their responses to them. Leaders who believe people are dependable create an aura of trust without even intending to do so. Likewise, leaders who believe that people are friendly are likely to find that, indeed, they are, because the leader's own behavior is open, straightforward, and warm. Leaders who do not believe people are friendly, on the other hand, approach them warily, tentatively, expecting resistance. People's reactions are very likely to confirm a leader's expectation. It is easy to explain our failures in human relationships by concentrating on what the other person did or did not do, when the real causes may lie in the behaviors produced by our own attitudes and beliefs.

The Leader's Self-Concept

According to perceptual-humanist thinking, people behave at any moment according to what they believe about themselves, the situations they confront, and the purposes they have in mind. Thus, what each of us believes about self is the most vital factor in determining behavior. How we see a situation may change from moment to moment. So may the purposes we are trying to fulfill. Beliefs about self, however, are always there, playing a major role in everything we do. Self-concepts are comparatively stable, the stars of every performance, the central figure around which all else revolves.

Self-concepts consist of the ways people perceive themselves, or the person and characteristics they refer to as *I* or *me*. Self-concepts begin to form very early in life. When babies are born, friends and relatives bring presents: blue ones for boys, pink ones for girls. Later, when little boys hurt themselves, they are told, "Boys don't cry!" When little girls hurt themselves, they usually are comforted and cuddled. So children learn very early that they are male or female and the "appropriate" behaviors for each role.

People learn who they are and what they are from the ways they are treated as they grow up. Over time, each of us develops thousands of self-definitions:

> My name is Sally Smith, I live in New York, I play the violin, I belong to the PTA, I can no longer wear a size 8.

We also learn to attach values to our definitions:

> I am happily married, a good cook, a fair tennis player, a smart businessman, and a rabid baseball fan.

The beliefs we have about ourselves also vary in importance. Self-concepts about which sex we represent are highly stable. We learned these very early and find them constantly corroborated by the worlds we inhabit. Other concepts do not seem so central to our personhood. All of us are aware of the little toe on the right foot, for example. We know it is part of us, but it plays hardly any role in our behavior—unless, perhaps, it gets stubbed.

Although self-concepts are central to behavior and have a high degree of stability, we can change them. Witness the changes as we grow older: I am a child, an adolescent, a young adult, a middle-aged adult, a senior citizen. Or, I am single, engaged, married, divorced. Generally speaking, the more important the concept of self and the longer it has been in existence, the more it resists change.

Any factor so important in human behavior must be of vital concern for educators. It is especially important that students develop positive views of themselves. Teachers and school leaders should develop positive views, too. Research shows that good teachers see themselves in positive ways (Combs, 1982). That means a major goal of education is helping teachers and students achieve positive feelings about self. But leaders, too, have self-concepts, and these are equally important in determining what they think and do. It makes a great deal of difference to their performance and success whether they perceive themselves as able or unable, adequate or inadequate. Leaders who see themselves as adequate to their tasks behave as such. They act with assurance and certainty. This helps those they work with to feel confidence in the leader. Leaders with doubts about themselves, on the other hand, are likely to act tentatively or fearfully. They engender feelings of anxiety or a lack of trust. Or, they may try so hard to give the impression that they are adequate that they overdo it, coming off more as braggarts than competent leaders. This also creates anxiety and undermines trust.

Whatever a leader's self-concept, those with whom the leader interacts will know it. As an old saying goes, "What you do speaks so loudly I cannot hear what you say." A leader's self-concept always shows, and coworkers can be heard saying: "Well, she would do that!" or "That's not what you can expect from him!" or "I can tell you right now what he will say about that." Educational leadership is not just a matter of what leaders do or say. It is also a question of who they are, a matter of their beliefs about themselves.

Once established, self-concepts tend to be self-fulfilling. People who see themselves as able, for example, behave as though they are. This very attitude increases their chances of being successful. Successful experience, in turn, simply confirms what they already believe: "I am enough. I am adequate to deal with the tasks I confront."

The self-corroborative character of self-concept is a matter of far-reaching consequences in U.S. culture. Millions of people are caught in a vicious circle of unfortunate beliefs about self. Believing they are only "X much," that is all they do. Others see them behaving so and evaluate them accordingly as, "Just an 'X much' person." This simply proves what the person thought in the first place. Perhaps you believe you cannot make a speech or you cannot "do math." The human and financial costs of such merry-go-rounds are incalculable. Much of the time and energies of educational leaders must be spent in helping students and faculties feel more competent and successful. How well leaders achieve such ends depends on the leaders' own self-concepts.

The Leader's Purposes

People behave in terms of how they see themselves, how they see the situations they confront, and the purposes they seek to fulfill. This is true for leaders as well. They behave according to their purposes at the moment they act. What is more, because our own purposes always have the feeling of being right or necessary at the moment we act, they have a feeling of certainty. This is true even when we misbehave or act stupidly or unwisely. Before the act, we may have been certain we would not behave so. After the act, we may be chagrined or embarrassed at what we did. But at the moment of acting, it seemed like a good, right, or necessary thing to do. It is an easy error to assume that others have the same goals we do. Consider the experience of one of this book's authors.

> Some years ago, Arthur Combs spoke to an audience that he was sure would be hostile to the position he was taking. Accordingly, he was fearful throughout the speech—and surprised at the audience's positive response at the end.
> Coming down from the stage, Combs met a colleague who said, "Art, don't you just love it when the spotlight is on you and there you are?" Combs looked at him in amazement. That wasn't at all how he felt! He was scared! A few minutes later, another friend made a fist and exclaimed, "Art, you really had 'em! You really did!" Near the back of the auditorium, Combs encountered a third colleague who remarked, "Very adroit, Art, very adroit!" as if Combs had just pulled off a neat intellectual trick.

> Each commentator responded to Combs's performance from his own frame of reference. Each assumed that Combs had the commentator's own purposes in making a speech: reveling in the limelight, relishing the feeling of power, or savoring the intellectual pleasure of "being adroit."

Acting on the assumption that others have the same experience, feelings, or beliefs as you can cause serious breakdowns in communication. It has frustrated many an attempt at educational reform. Though we may share purposes with others on some occasions, the particular pattern of people's purposes is always highly unique. Whatever the leader's purposes, they determine behavior. Just as coworkers read a leader's beliefs about people, so too they generally can infer the nature of a leader's purposes.

Purposes vary widely from moment to moment. Some are fleeting, but others are so important that they seem basic to a person's very existence. How and when purposes show up in behavior is a matter of their importance in the person's belief system. Indeed, many of the failures or embarrassing dilemmas that leaders face are a consequence of failure to determine what is important. Without a clear perception of what is truly important, leaders can easily get caught up in a merry-go-round that goes like this:

> Because I do not know what is important, everything is important. Since everything is important, I have to do everything. Because I keep trying to do everything, people see me doing everything, and then they expect me to do everything. That keeps me so busy I do not have time to think about what is important!

This vicious circle is responsible for the problems and failures of people everywhere. It can be particularly devastating for people in leadership positions.

Research shows that one of the major purposes associated with effective helpers is that good helpers tend to be freeing rather than controlling (Combs & Avila, 1985). They want to set teachers, students, clients, patients, or parishioners free. Poor helpers seek to control, direct, and manage those with whom they work. Good helpers also are more concerned with people than things. What happens to people is their primary concern. Poor helpers concentrate so intensely on things—rules, regulations, forms, or organization, for example— that they forget they are working with people. Likewise, good helpers' purposes tend to be broad rather than narrow. Poor performers become preoccupied with details to the exclusion of larger goals.

In addition to such major purposes, leaders behave in many more ways pertaining to all aspects of their work. Some are personal, related to their own needs, aspirations, hopes, fears, loves, hates, and goals. Others are social, philosophical, or professional. The latter, of course, have great importance for leaders' behaviors. It makes a great deal of difference what leaders believe about the goals of education. For example, is the purpose of high school to prepare students for college, or is the purpose to help all students to achieve the maximum of their potential? Are parents a necessary evil, or should they be involved in planning and action? Should teachers be free to make their own plans, or should they be required to stick to the text? Should they be involved in decision making, or is that the prerogative of administration? Whatever leaders believe is important surely will be revealed in their behavior.

The Leader's Authenticity

Everyone, including leaders, exhibits two kinds of behaviors. There are those things we do to cope with life, to manage the events we confront. Each of us also behaves expressively. These are the things we do, almost without thinking, that are simple expressions of who we are and how we feel at any moment. Coping behavior requires conscious manipulation of people, objects, or events to accomplish an objective. Coping behaviors represent attempts to do what we ought to, should, or must do to achieve a desired end. Expressive behaviors, on the other hand, require no such forethought or management. They simply happen as a consequence of feelings or beliefs existing at a given moment.

You cannot have a relationship with a nonentity. Effective people have to be somebody. People with well-developed belief systems who see themselves in positive ways and who feel comfortable with who they are do very little coping. Instead, simply by expressing, they cope. They act authentically, and they are who they are without effort. People around them see the things they do and say as natural, unaffected, and totally appropriate.

People are authentic as a product of their belief systems. It is no small accomplishment to possess a comprehensive and trustworthy belief system with a deep understanding of its supporting data. It is an experiential achievement that can give order and unity to the person and his or her impact on those with whom he or she interacts.

Research on good helpers reports that effective practitioners are self-revealing; poor practitioners are self-concealing. Better performers are more authentic, more capable of being who they are without pretense or the need to hide behind psychological defenses. These findings are corroborated by research results on effective counselors and psychotherapists. Good helpers in those professions are able to be open, transparently themselves.

That kind of authenticity is a valuable trait for leaders. It promotes a feeling of trust among colleagues and coworkers. People feel more secure with such leaders. They see such leaders as solid, confident, and self-assured. People who are not authentic give the impression that they are "acting" their roles, playing games, and being false.

It can be very frustrating to work with a boss or supervisor who pretends to be what he or she is not. You can never find out how to reach such a person. If you treat the boss the way you know he or she really is from your observations, the boss rejects you. This person also may become annoyed or angry because you have not treated him or her the way he or she is pretending to be. To treat the boss in the way he or she desires, you must play act, pretending something you do not feel. Either way of responding does not feel right, and it leaves people confused. In such dilemmas, people stay as far away from the boss as possible, avoiding interaction of any kind.

Authenticity, of course, is the external manifestation of a person's belief system. People who are authentic are at peace with themselves. They see themselves in positive ways; have clear perceptions of reality; and operate from belief systems that are comprehensive, accurate, and internally consistent. Such belief systems provide trustworthy guidelines for action. They produce effective, stable behavior with a minimum of contradictions. That, in turn, contributes to feelings of trust, lowered levels of anxiety, greater levels of confidence, and cooperation.

For many years, educational leaders have concentrated on "things" in the profession. We now recognize that educational leadership is overwhelmingly a human problem, and we are looking to modern perceptual-experiential thinking to design a person-centered perspective. From a person-centered viewpoint, the causes of behavior, including a leader's behaviors, are found in people's belief systems. Effective leadership is a function of the leader's personal system of beliefs. The making of a leader, then, is a problem of being and becoming, the continual refinement of a leader's beliefs about self, the world, and the job.

To some, defining effective leadership in terms of a leader's belief system may seem a flimsy basis for professional practice. This may be true if a leader's belief system is shoddy, weak, inaccurate, or full of inconsistencies. However, a belief system that is comprehensive, accurate, defensible, internally consistent, and continuously subject to review and adaptation deserves to be trusted. It can provide both order and harmony to a leader's performance and a dependable frame of reference for working helpfully and responsibly as a true professional.

In this chapter we have focused on the personal aspects of the leader's belief system with special reference to research findings on good and poor helpers and the fundamental significance of human belief systems in determining human behavior. A leader's success also depends on how well he or she works with others. Since people behave according to their perceptions or beliefs, it follows that how teachers teach and students learn is a function of their belief systems. Thus, successful educational leadership also depends on the leader's ability to facilitate the growth and development of teachers, staff members, and students. The next chapter is devoted to exploring basic principles about the kind of data person-centered leaders need to fulfill this role.

SEEKING AND
RESPONDING TO DATA

THIS CHAPTER FOCUSES ON ONE EDUCATIONAL LEADER
in particular: the principal—though in this era of shared decision
making, our observations and recommendations apply to people in
many other roles, as well. Principals' responsibilities are immense and
diverse, and their lives are filled with details. They deal with everything from broken boilers to distraught parents, from angry cooks to
state championship tennis players to new history standards. From
morning until sometimes late into the night, they interact constantly
with the people and things of their organization: students, parents,
teachers, central office staff, community leaders, state board in-
spectors, university students and supervisors, vendors, social service agencies, college admission officers, gymnasiums, buses, floors,
doors, food, curriculum mandates, purchase orders, textbooks, library
books, parking, achievement tests, bathrooms.

Sometimes, the sheer volume of data that principals must respond
to seems overwhelming (Miser, 1995). One researcher found that on
the average, a principal engages in 50 tasks per hour, with each task
lasting an average of one to two minutes (Peterson, 1981). A princi-

pal's job demands that he or she be prepared to respond to hundreds of pieces of data every day. Discussion of these data, therefore, is important to any consideration of effective leadership.

Distinguishing Types of Data

Principals usually come from the ranks of teachers. As former teachers, they are familiar with the performance and behavior data used to evaluate students' growth. However, other data are significant to principals. In Chapter 1, we shared one factor that distinguishes effective and ineffective helpers: the kind of data that the helpers seek and respond to (Combs, 1986). In a people-intensive organization like a school, an effective leader will seek and respond, for the most part, to data about people. Things may require the principal's management skills, but people are the most significant part of the school. They require the principal's best leadership skills. It is mostly these issues with people that affect the school's success or failure.

Yet in their graduate programs, future school leaders mostly learn about the "things" of their work. For example, a future principal will study finance and budgeting, school law, management, governance, auxiliary and support services, curriculum and instruction, organizational theory, and supervision and evaluation. Although some of this curriculum focuses on people, much of the content addresses data related to "things."

This content certainly is important for principals to know, because they are held accountable for budgets, boilers, lockers, buses, clean floors, and legal procedures. Nevertheless, school principals work in an organization where the products of the work are people—students—and where students' welfare is the major goal. The principalship is a job where the most important part of the work is people, not things. In fact, many principals rue the time taken away from people by the things-related details that drive their everyday existence (Miser, 1995).

This new concept of leadership requires a redirection of leaders' attention. They must attend less to "things" and more to people. This concept rejects the idea that leadership is the manipulation and control of people to change their behavior to fit a leader's goal. Instead, effective leaders immerse themselves in the work lives of the people they are leading, becoming sensitive to what they think and how they perceive things.

Attending to Different Data

A person-centered approach to leadership presumes that leaders are sensitive to the meaning of people's behavior; they avoid focusing on the behavior itself. Principals don't need to pay attention to the meaning of broken lockers and dirty floors. Broken lockers require direct action on their hinges, locks, or doors, and dirty floors require a good cleaning. But when interactions with people are broken or "dirty," the actions required to repair the break or cleanse the "dirt" are not so simple or direct. Prevention strategies aren't so simple, either.

Effective principals learn to interpret the meanings of people's behavior. They recognize that behavior is not a direct response to an external situation. Instead, behavior is a response filtered through each individual's perception of a situation. Effective leaders know that behavior is merely a symptom of the beliefs and perceptions another person holds. Whether that person is a student, parent, teacher, community leader, or supervisor, he or she will interact with the principal based on what he or she believes to be true of the situation. In other words, our behavior merely reflects our perception of a situation and what kind of action—or inaction—we believe the situation requires.

What does it mean when we say effective leaders deal with the meanings of behavior rather than the behavior itself? It means that what happens is not as important as what people feel and think about what happens. A principal's effectiveness, therefore, will be related directly to how sensitive he or she is to the feelings and thoughts of others and how well the principal can communicate that sensitivity to others. It means that to be effective, a leader must be aware of what people think and feel about what happens in the school, and the leader needs to learn to respond accordingly.

School leaders frequently interact with others to resolve a conflict or make a decision about a course of action. In these situations, effective leaders "read behavior backward" to understand what beliefs people hold about themselves and a situation. This ability to read behavior backward allows principals to reach a better decision about a course of action, "better" meaning a decision that meets the needs of as many individuals as possible. "Reading behavior backward" is another way of saying that a good leader develops and extends the empathy that he or she has for others. A good leader also learns to express that empathy in ways that benefit the individuals involved and, consequently, the school and students.

For an example of reading behavior backward, let's look at what could be a typical interaction for any principal walking down a school hallway.

A principal is stopped in the hallway by Tom, a new teacher in the building.

"Did you hear about the phone call that I got from Debbie's mother?" Tom asks, obviously still upset and flustered. The principal responds that she hasn't heard about the phone call. Tom goes on to explain that Debbie's mother thinks his choice of novels is inappropriate, and she has forbidden Debbie to read the assigned book.

The principal responds, "What did you say to Debbie's mother?"

"I told her that Debbie had to read the book because it was a class requirement. I also told her that I had selected the books for my class carefully and that all of them were appropriate for adolescents. I also said that if she had a problem with that, she should call you. After she slammed the phone down on me, I went to find Dan [the department chair] to see if what I said was okay. He said it was, but that I should tell you just in case the mother calls you. I was just on my way to the office right now." Tom casts a worried look at the principal.

Just then the department chair comes down the hall, sees the two talking, and walks over to join the conversation.

"I told Tom that he has my support and that he would have your support on this, too. I know that you believe in teachers having final say-so in their classrooms," says Dan.

The principal replies that they should get together after school to talk about the situation when it's calmer and quieter. Having forgotten where she originally was going, she heads back to the office.

On her desk she finds a message that Debbie's mother has called. Debbie's mother wants to let the principal know that she has been insulted by one of her daughter's teachers and is coming in after school to talk about it. She also is calling her school board representative about the attitude of teachers at the school and how they think they are "gods" and never listen to parents. The principal shakes her head as she realizes that what might have been a simple encounter is going to turn into a complicated disagreement involving more people than it ever needed to.

How would an effective leader respond to this situation so that all parties involved feel the conflict is resolved reasonably and equitably—and the student's welfare remains the primary goal?

Examining Option 1

Let's review the facts. The principal knows that the new teacher made a mistake, though it seems evident that the teacher does not know that. School policy allows for parents to request an alternative assignment if a novel chosen for a class violates some family or religious value, which can be demonstrated through the parent's written analysis of sections of the novel. Tom, the teacher, should have explained this policy to the mother and invited her to come in to complete the necessary forms. The principal also knows that Dan, the department chair, is quite familiar with this policy. The mother clearly is upset and angry, enough so that she is getting a school board member involved. This encounter is on the heels of a two-year, schoolwide effort to foster closer ties between the school and families and to involve parents more in their students' education. The principal also suspects that the student, Debbie, might not have any idea what is going on.

The principal has several options. She could attempt to manipulate externally the forces at play. For example, she could reprimand the new teacher and tell him to read the faculty/staff handbook more closely. She could require him to call the mother, apologize, and go over the policy with her. The principal could chide the department chair for failing to notify new faculty in his department about school policies, especially ones that can cause friction between the school and parents. She also could take exception to the fact that the chair set her up to look bad with the new teacher, knowing that she would be unable to support his actions. She could phone Debbie's mother and negotiate with her not to call the school board member if Debbie is allowed to avoid reading the book.

What would result if the principal chose these options? Probably it would be the first and last time the new teacher ever brought a concern to the principal, since the principal has chosen to be punitive about his behavior rather than understanding. Probably the principal would lose the support of the department chair on future issues because she has chosen to chastise him rather than empathize with his desire to lead a good department and to be proud of the activities of the teachers in that department. The mother would learn that if you protest loudly enough and threaten to go to higher authorities, you can get what you want. The principal's actions would reinforce the notion of parental blackmail, rather than cooperative problem solving, to meet students' needs. The student would learn that the principal is swayed easily and fears confrontation and conflict—and that the authority of teacher expertise might not be supported in the school. If they found out about the incident, which is likely, the board member and the superintendent would learn that the principal cannot be trusted to inform them of important issues if they might cast a negative light on the school.

Examining Option 2

Instead of responding to the overt behavior of the people involved and her need to be in control of the school, however, the principal could opt to begin the process of resolution by "reading behavior backward," by attempting to understand the thinking and perceptions of the people involved. If she chooses this option she will seek the meanings being attached to this situation by all the participants so that she can understand what happened from all perspectives. Let's see how the principal does this.

> The principal begins with Debbie since she has no idea where the student stands on all this or even if she knows what is happening. She asks her secretary to track down Debbie and bring her in before the end of school so that she can find out her feelings on the issue. The principal believes strongly that students should have appropriate input in their education, and she believes that Debbie is mature enough to have an educated and involved opinion on this matter, an opinion that needs to be honored and respected. She hopes that Debbie's mother has talked this matter over with her, but her experience tells her that may not be the case.
>
> Next, the principal faces the issues that probably will arise with the teacher, Tom. She heard uncertainty and tentativeness in his voice—and the hope that he did what was right. She also saw the look of worry on his face and heard his distress about the encounter with Debbie's mother. The principal decides that she must alleviate the new teacher's concern by somehow supporting him while at the same time upholding the school policy. She decides to focus on all the things that Tom did right: plan his curriculum carefully, choose his materials thoughtfully, make himself available to a student's parent, notify his department chair, and follow up by letting the principal know about a potential problem. Then she decides to enlist his support in working with the mother on the school policy. In this way, he will have to learn the policy himself.
>
> Rather than chastise Tom for giving inaccurate information to the mother, this principal reinforces his thoughtful planning, his willingness to discuss issues with the parents of his students, his thoughtfulness about checking with his department chair before going any further,

and his following through on letting the principal know about a potential conflict with a parent. The principal also shows Tom the school's regulations regarding parents' challenges to curriculum choices and the procedures in place to handle such complaints so that he can make a more informed response next time. She gives Tom the proper forms and lets him decide how he would like to contact the parent. She offers to meet with them or to have the department chair meet with them if Tom would feel more comfortable with that arrangement. The principal's major concern is to let Tom know that his professional responsibility and his courteous treatment of a parent are valued, that it is okay not to know every single policy about a new school, and that she has confidence that through problem solving he can rectify the situation with the parent. In this way, the principal alleviates some of the uncertainty she heard in the new teacher's voice and, through joint problem solving, helps him look at alternatives for handling similar concerns in the future.

Next the principal turns to the mother. Clearly, the mother is angry and will not want to wait while the principal meets with Tom and the department chair after school. The principal decides to telephone the mother to allow her a chance to vent her anger and to explain her side of what happened. The principal hopes that by listening to the mother immediately she will be able to hold off on the requested meeting until the next morning, after she has had a chance to talk to Debbie and to the teacher and department chair. The mother agrees to a meeting before school starts the next day, when the principal will have more information to share with her. The principal apologizes for any suggestion of insulting behavior and assures the mother that her concerns will be heard by everyone, that the teacher did not mean to insult her, and that any decision will be made in her daughter's best interest. She reminds the mother that the school is committed to working with parents as partners in the educational process and commends the mother for calling about her concern rather than just being quietly frustrated. She asks the mother to talk to her daughter that night to see how she feels about the issue and suggests that Debbie should be included in the meeting the next morning.

The principal knows the school board member well enough to expect that this kind of issue is one that will probably get an emotional response. Therefore, she calls the superintendent to let her know what is brewing and asks if she would like for her to call the school board member. The superintendent replies that she will go ahead and call since she has another reason to phone anyway. She promises to get back to the principal if it looks like there might be a problem. The superintendent also thanks the principal for letting her know ahead of time about a potential "hot potato."

Next is the most problematic of the people issues: reading backward the behavior of the department chair. His behavior has in some ways set up the principal to look bad in the eyes of a new teacher. Dan knows there are specific policies regarding challenges to curriculum materials, yet evidently he has not informed Tom of these policies nor has he referred to them in his conversation with him about Debbie's mother. Dan has told Tom that he is sure the principal will uphold his decision to require the book, even though he knows that sometimes the principal cannot do that and instead must help find an alternative choice. Contradicting the new teacher's decision will make the principal look as if she is not in favor of teacher autonomy, something Dan knows is not true. The principal is a bit confused by all this. She is sure that Dan knows the policies, and she has never had an experience with Dan where he was anything but competent and professional.

The principal puzzles over the meaning of Dan's behavior. She decides that possibly he is feeling bad and a little guilty that he hasn't informed the new teacher of what to do in cases like this and is trying to prevent himself and his department from looking bad in the eyes of the principal. It is the only meaning that she can think of that would make sense.

She decides to ignore her own need for school department chairs to be informed about and supportive of school policies and walks down to Dan's office to talk with him before school is out. She tells Dan about her conversation with Debbie's mother and laughs with him about how quickly small things can turn big. She recalls with him a past event when something tiny turned into a giant brouhaha, and they both grin at the recollection of how that mess finally got resolved.

The principal then thanks Dan for advising the teacher to inform her about what was happening and thanks him for being supportive of a new teacher who was uncertain about what course of action to take. Then she decides to problem solve with Dan about how they might best support Tom and still get across the information that he needs to make a more informed decision next time. She asks advice from Dan about how to best proceed with the parent and invites him to the morning meeting. She tells Dan that she could use his level head and support in the meeting if he would be willing to come in a little early. The principal then asks Dan if there is anything she can do to help him with Tom. Dan looks relieved, thanks the principal, and says he thinks everything is under control and that he can work with Tom to look for some alternative choice of book if need be. He also assures the principal that both he and Tom will be at the meeting tomorrow to work out the situation with Debbie and her mother.

This principal exemplifies how an effective leader would use the skill of reading behavior backward, or empathy, to determine the needs of all the individuals involved and to plan how all these needs can be met to the greatest extent possible. She realizes that

- supporting a new teacher's early efforts to be professional is more important than telling him to read the handbook more carefully,
- supporting a mother's concern about her daughter is more important than defending the actions of the school,
- informing the superintendent and board member to allow them some time to think about the issue is more important than keeping the conflict from them, and
- reinforcing the leadership and collaboration of the department chair is more important than telling him how annoyed she is that he "set her up."

This principal can engage in all these actions because of the data she sought and the data she chose to ignore. She sought people's perceptions by thinking about what their behaviors might indicate, and she responded to the meaning of those perceptions. She ignored the behavior itself, even when the behavior annoyed her or challenged something about the school for which she was responsible. Her main concern was, "What does all this mean to each of these players, and how can I help resolve this situation so that everyone is heard and respected?"

The chances of this conflict being resolved successfully seem high, thanks to this leader's ability to empathize with the people involved, to understand the meaning underlying each person's behavior, to set aside personal needs, and to respond to the needs of the people involved. Her actions will make it possible for the new teacher, department chair, mother, and student to grow positively from the experience. The new teacher will feel supported and will learn firsthand about the school policy. The department chair will feel supported and needed rather than reprimanded. The mother will feel that the school hears her voice. The student will have a chance to give important input on how she believes the issue can be resolved in her best interest.

Expanding Empathy

Effective leadership means that leaders expand their capacity for empathy to include everyone with whom they interact. People have a tendency to restrict their empathy to those who are like themselves or to those they love and care about. Principals are no different. But good leaders learn to expand their empathy to include those who are unlike themselves, to those who are culturally and economically different from them, to those who are low-achieving and undercommitted to school, to those who resent and challenge the leader's authority, to those who lack confidence, to those whose welfare is in the hands of others, and to those who seem to act in ways that do not further students' interests. In other words, they use empathy with those who are very different from themselves.

School leaders interact with a broad spectrum of people, including people of all ages. They must understand the perceptions of adults *and* children. Children's meanings about things sometimes are quite different from those assigned by adults. Yet school leaders are held accountable for all that happens in the school, even though they have little direct control over what happens in classrooms or hallways, on the playground, in the lunchroom, or on the fields or courts where student activities occur.

Frequently, leaders find themselves in situations where they must arbitrate conflicts without firsthand knowledge of the events and without the luxury of time to investigate the situation. They must act empathetically to the immediate and pressing needs of the people involved. In addition, these situations tend to occur in a public setting, usually in an atmosphere of high emotion. Responding only to behavior can escalate the situation to an even higher level of conflict. For example, what might have happened with Tom and Dan if the principal chose to be angry and punitive? Responding empathetically to the meanings people assign to a situation decreases the level of conflict and allows for a more measured and reflective solution among all participants.

Considering the sheer number of interactions that characterize a leader's work, this requirement that they be sensitive to the perceptions of others can be exhausting. Extending empathy to all people requires the leader to display personal discipline and develop a "thick skin." It requires taking the time needed to meet people's needs, and time is a precious commodity to busy administrators. It requires the suppression of personal needs, beliefs, and feelings in favor of the needs, beliefs, and feelings of others. It requires consciously seeking out those we might otherwise ignore or overlook, particularly those who do not find the school setting a place that enhances their individuality and talents. This people-intensive work is demanding, and it can take a toll on every school leader.

Another requirement of this kind of empathy is that leaders must be aware of how their own behavior illustrates the meanings underlying that behavior. Effective leaders will discipline themselves to engage in behavior that has consistent meaning and direction rather than random eclecticism. People within the school need to know and understand the meanings of the principal's behavior if they are to be able to predict it. If people can't predict how a leader is going to behave, they will avoid that person. Effective school leaders, there-fore, seek ways to find out what people are thinking and feeling and will find frequent opportunities to clarify their own belief systems for others. Effective leaders make their belief systems and personal mean-ings known and also reflect on and share with others the constant evolution of their personal belief systems.

Creating Empathic School Environments

The notion of empathy is not limited to interactions with people. Empathic leaders also can create a compassionate and sensitive school environment. Policies and practices will assure that all students, staff, and parents are treated with equity and care, or policies and practices will create a school environment characterized by divisiveness, injus-tice, and alienation. The curriculum has the potential to allow for, and even encourage, students and teachers to expand their empathy and their understanding of differing perspectives. It is easy for school leaders to verbalize empathy for others; it is harder for leaders to examine all the practices and content of the school to find ways to extend and expand empathic responses and understanding.

For example, in most schools, teachers are asked to nominate students for awards. An empathic leader will put into place a selection procedure that closely monitors the diversity of students receiving awards, paying particular attention to gender and ethnic diversity and whether students with disabilities are included for consideration. Research shows that boys tend to get more attention in schools than girls and that Anglo students get more positive attention than stu-dents of color or students with disabilities (Sadker & Sadker, 1994). Without a sensitive monitoring system in place, it would be possible for awards to be distributed mostly to Anglo boys. Other equally deserving students might unconsciously get overlooked by even a well-intentioned faculty.

An empathic leader could meet parents' needs to be equal partners in the school process by conveniently scheduling alternate meeting times for parents who must work night shifts or depend on older children to watch younger siblings. Also, school leaders could schedule meetings in the community so that transportation need not be a concern. Or, they could make arrangements for school-bus pickups at various places in the community on the afternoons or nights of parent meetings so that parents without cars can get to the school.

Principals can extend their empathy into students' extracurricular programs by encouraging coaches to be sensitive to cultural differences when setting dress codes for teams so they don't exclude students of an ethnic or economic minority from participating. Athletic policies that require young men to cut their hair short, for example, could prevent some Native American or African American students from participating. Requirements to purchase expensive equipment or pay for meals at games away from home could prevent economically disadvantaged students from participating. Mandatory practices or meetings on non-Christian holidays could exclude some students from participating. An effective leader educates faculty sponsors and coaches about these potential obstacles and helps them develop procedures that are sensitive to these issues so as many students as possible are included in school activities.

School leaders also can promote policies that assure advanced-level classes are available to all students. Typically, the prerequisites for entrance into these types of programs favor white students from economically advantaged families. In reality, there are as many gifted students in all ethnic and economic groups. A sensitive and empathic leader will look for bias in the systems schools use to identify potential participants in enrichment activities and work with the faculty to eliminate those biases.

School leaders who are empathic to all cultures also can encourage music, art, and drama programs to reflect a diversity that is sensitive to and respectful of the contributions of all cultures, not just the majority culture. By working with faculty, students, and parents, empathic principals can raise the awareness level of everyone in the school to include many cultures' views. Because the arts offer such a rich heritage from all cultures, literature, drama, music, and art are easy avenues for the celebration of diverse backgrounds and histories. In a school where people are empathic to all students, winter concerts that include musical offerings from around the world replace Christmas music programs. All-school assemblies become opportunities to learn about other cultures' customs and stories. Literature classes reflect the works of authors who beautifully convey life in the world outside the Western, European experience.

Other areas of the school's curriculum also can encourage the extension and expansion of empathy. For example, academic assignments can expand students' sensitivity to the needs of all people. Imagine seeing the Revolutionary War through the eyes of Tory children who lived in Boston. Or imagine hearing the stories of slaves of northern Civil War leaders who publicly proclaimed emancipation but privately owned personal slaves. Such activities allow students to put themselves into the minds of others and understand their experiences, but these activities frequently are forgotten in the interest of "covering" all the material. In addition, community service offers opportunities for students to act on the moral consciences they are expanding and extending through their classroom studies. These opportunities also allow for closer connections between students and their neighbors. Service activities let students expand their concepts of themselves as "helping selves," and they lay the foundation for students to become empathic, caring adults who are deeply involved in their communities.

The avenues for creating an empathic and caring environment are nearly endless. Good leaders seize these avenues to help others learn to care about and understand a variety of viewpoints. It is the leader's responsibility to monitor the system and all the assumptions underlying it, watching for ways that the school can be more inclusive of and sensitive to all students, families, and staff members.

Understanding the Costs of Empathic Leadership

Effective leaders are committed to seeking meaning in all the behaviors of the people in the school and in all the activities that characterize the school's operation. These meanings are the data that effective leaders seek. There is, however, a high price to searching out these types of data and responding to them: time and personal energy.

Becoming an empathic leader requires that leaders do extra work. Rather than just responding to situations at face value, leaders must take the time to uncover what is really going on in the minds of all involved. They must give up time for responding to other things, things that are probably easier, more tangible, and sometimes even more satisfying. It means that principals have to become more reflective. They have to spend more time with people, quality time, not just time for casual conversation. They have to restrain their own needs in favor of the needs of others. They have to be on call for others. They have to hone their empathic skills so they can respond sensitively to others. They have to be on constant guard against their tendency to respond to things only through their own eyes.

Empathic leadership also takes personal commitment. It requires that leaders have personal clarity about and confidence in their own beliefs, behavior, and abilities. At the same time, however, they must keep only a tentative hold on beliefs, realizing that what they know and believe today may not be what they will know and believe tomorrow. This kind of clarity demands personal honesty, which is gained through hours of personal reflection. The confidence that effective leaders convey comes from knowing that they have thoughtfully sought the best possible data about people, and they have made decisions based on what they believe to be true about people based on that data. This is not confidence that comes from leaders knowing that they are "always" right. With so many individuals' perceptions and needs to be taken into account, only the rare leader would believe with absolute certainty that he or she has always done the right thing. What is more important is that the person-centered leader consciously seeks out significant data—the meaning of behavior—and consciously puts aside the less significant data—the behavior itself.

Because of the need for great sensitivity and empathy, effective leaders also must have a certain tolerance for ambiguity. They must have confidence in and clarity about beliefs that guide their practice while at the same time they must encourage and listen to others who do not necessarily agree with those beliefs. Principals walk a tightrope between being empathic and being managerial when facing adults who seem to have agendas other than students' best interests at heart. Principals often evaluate the work of adults who do not engage in best practice because they do not know best practice, because they have personal needs that get in the way of carrying out best practice, or because some other motivation is greater than that to meet students' needs. When to be firmly managerial and when to be empathic is a question not easily answered by school leaders who care deeply for others and respect their viewpoints.

These vast demands that school leaders be empathic beg for outlets for principals. They need places where they can ventilate their frustrations without harming the school or their relationships with others. They also need to experience firsthand the same kind of empathic understanding they offer to others. The fact that these outlets rarely are built into the school system is another price that effective leaders pay for their work.

When school leaders find themselves floating alone, swamped by a sea of unyielding demands, they need some sort of "life preserver." Principals have the same needs for empathic understanding that others do. They must seek networks of people who will offer them that understanding and who will help replenish their drained energy. Knowledge of one's own needs is important, and effective leaders seek the same data about themselves as they do for others: What am I feeling? How am I thinking about this? Why do I feel this way? What meaning does all this have for me as a person and a leader? Leaders must attend to their own needs if they are to take care of others' needs, too.

❧ ❧ ❧

Is the toll worth it? Each leader must answer that question individually. The kind of leadership that is required in schools today is not easy, nor is it always clear and tidy. Paying attention to the meanings of others' behavior requires a different kind of energy and commitment from a leader than does paying attention to the "things" of the organization.

In the long run, it is leadership that can inspire others to greater personal and professional satisfaction and achievement. It is leadership that can energize a school to recognize and honor the needs, dignity, and abilities of all people. The result is schools where people grow and flourish, practice newfound skills and competencies, and gain the confidence and knowledge to become healthy, contributing adults.

II

LEADERS' CONCEPTIONS OF CHANGE AND SELF

3
BELIEFS ABOUT PEOPLE
AND CHANGE

WHAT YOU BELIEVE ABOUT THE NATURE OF PEOPLE AND their motivation in life has far-reaching consequences for how you approach leadership tasks and relationships. For example, in a things-oriented culture, motivation usually is defined as what we do to get people to behave in the manner we desire. Actually, getting people to behave the way we want is not motivation; it is management, control, or manipulation. Much of traditional educational leadership has proceeded from this perspective.

Another very old idea about human motivation is the doctrine of original sin, which holds that people are basically sinful, depraved, evil, untrustworthy, and inherently inclined to behave badly. The essential goal of life, therefore, is to achieve salvation. A leader's task is to make sure that goal is achieved. With such beliefs in mind, it is not surprising that early schools were very grim places. They had to be: Salvation was at stake! These beliefs about human motivation were current for hundreds of years, and many people even today still share them.

Many others still hold to a concept of human nature and motivation that views people as battlegrounds. According to this viewpoint, people constantly are engaged in a struggle between good and evil. This was the basic concept of psychoanalysis, which regarded personality as the outgrowth of conflict between the id (the dark forces of one's character) and the superego (the higher values of society). However, modern, person-centered psychology offers different and more promising viewpoints than all these perspectives.

The Person-Centered View

In recent years, a more positive understanding of human relationships has been supplied by perceptual-experiential psychology's concept of motivation (Combs & Gonzalez, 1997). This view holds that human beings are born neither good nor evil, nor are they constantly at war within themselves. At birth, they just are. In later life, they might be judged as good or evil, but they were not born so.

This is not to say that humans are passive or without direction. Quite the contrary. From the moment of conception, we begin an insatiable reach for wholeness or health that never ceases until death has occurred in the last cell. This is sometimes called "the growth principle." This fundamental need is characteristic of protoplasm itself, the stuff of life. The drive toward health is a built-in quality of every living cell, including the millions that make up a human being.

People can, will, and must move toward health—*if* the way seems open for them to do so. The practice of medicine is built on this principle. Doctors do not cure us. They minister to the body by prescribing rest, medication, or nutrition; eliminating germs; or removing an offending organ. They help the body cure itself. Counselors and teachers also rely on this fundamental human need as they try to help clients or students grow. They cannot make people solve problems or learn. They can only facilitate the processes by which clients or students discover more effective ways of seeking personal fulfillment.

Maintenance and Enhancement of Self

More specifically, person-centered thinking tells us that human beings differ from most other animals in that what we strive for much more than the maintenance of our physical bodies. Instead, we seek to maintain and enhance the self, the being we refer to as "I" or "me."

Our self-concepts ride around in our physical bodies, but they are much more important than the vehicle they inhabit. We are quite willing, for example, to risk our physical bodies for the sake of maintaining or enhancing our personal self. If we just wanted to maintain our bodies, we would never drive too fast; eat too much; or ingest alcohol, drugs, or tobacco. Knowing what we do about the transmission of disease, of course, we would never kiss or hug another person. Yet we do all those things, and people often are willing to sacrifice their physical selves for all sorts of causes. For example, people will die for their loved ones or for their nation in a time of war. Even suicide becomes comprehensible when it is viewed as a means to join one's ancestors, to avoid disgrace, or to escape from intolerable emotional pain.

This fundamental need for maintenance and enhancement of the self means that people are always motivated. Indeed, people are never unmotivated. The young boy spending his time in history class teasing the girl who sits in front of him is not unmotivated; he just isn't motivated to do what his teacher thinks is important!

At first glance it may seem distasteful that we are all motivated by the need to maintain and enhance our selves. You might ask, "Whatever happened to altruism, love, and unselfishness?" Actually, nobility and altruism are still alive and well in the capacity of the self-concept to include others. As children grow, they learn to feel "one with" their mothers, fathers, siblings, and playmates. We hope that when they grow older, they identify with their school and later with their social clubs, religion, ethnic group, or nation. Self-actualized people even may achieve a feeling of being one with all humankind, or the universe itself. When the self has expanded to include others, what one does for self is done for others as well. Likewise, what one does for others is for self, too.

This person-centered view of humanity has far-reaching implications for leadership. Seeing people as basically motivated toward health calls for a quite different approach than exerting force for management and control. It requires a way of working with people's built-in needs rather than opposing or controlling them. It calls for leaders who see themselves as helpers and facilitators rather than directors or managers.

The Power of Need

A human's basic need for maintenance and self-enhancement is so fundamental that it cannot be set aside except for very short periods. Many of the difficulties encountered in education are consequences of trying to motivate people to learn or change when they see no relationship between what they are asked to do and their personal need. Donald Snygg once expressed it, "The trouble with American education is that we are, all of us, giving people answers to problems they don't have yet" (personal communication, 1962). To this we can now add, "And may never have."

Teachers and administrators assume that students and coworkers need this or that information, or, if they don't, they should! But working with human need instead of against it leaves two options for motivation:

• Leaders and teachers can create a need before offering workers or students information. That is essentially what is attempted with reward or punishment.

• Leaders and teachers can involve the needs of those with whom they work by relating information to the person's existing need. By all odds, the simpler, speedier, and more efficient road to motivation is to use an already existing personal need.

Though the concept of need is important for the learning process, few schools give more than lip-service to the notion. The curriculum is delivered to students whether they have any need for it or not. It is human nature to seek out what we need and avoid groups that are not personally fulfilling. It is no accident that a major complaint of high school students is, "School is so irrelevant!"

The concept of need and motivation we have outlined here has far-reaching implications for educational leadership. Education is essentially a people business. It depends on the interaction of people at every level, including students, teachers, counselors, supervisors, maintenance or administrative staffs, school boards, parents, and legislators. How effectively leaders interact with all these people and, in turn, how effectively they facilitate the interaction of those people will determine success or failure. Educational leaders must recognize this concept and adapt to its implications. To ignore it is like saying, "I know my car needs a carburetor, but I'm going to drive without one!"

Challenge and Threat

Challenge and threat also have important implications for people's basic needs for maintenance and self-enhancement. People feel challenged when they are confronted with matters that interest them and that they believe they have a chance of resolving. People feel threatened when they are confronted with events they do not feel they can handle (see Caine & Caine, 1991).

This distinction has ramifications for everyone engaged in education, especially for leaders. When people feel challenged, they are

highly motivated, ready to engage in activities with vigor and concentration. The situation is quite different when people feel threatened. Threat results in two very negative consequences.

Threat and Self-Defense

The first consequence of threat is mobilization for self-defense.
When people feel threatened, the need for maintenance and enhancement leads them to strenuous self-defense. We have all seen
this behavior in ourselves and others. The more people are threatened, the more strongly they rally to the defense of their precious
selves. The hotter the argument gets, the more protagonists stick to
the positions they held in the first place.

This need for self-defense generates conflict. The scenario goes
like this: Person A makes a statement. Person B sees this statement
as threatening. In self-defense, B retorts with a threatening statement,
which is seen by A as both threatening and unreasonable. Accordingly, Person A lets fly with a more scorching response, which Person
B experiences as outrageous. Person B is now so irate, he or she attacks
Person A viciously. Person A, of course, cannot brook such insult and
responds in kind, only more so. This infuriates Person B, who hauls
off and socks Person A. So a great battle begins.

This escalating interaction of threat and counterthreat is characteristic of most conflict situations. If not interrupted somewhere
along the line, it may continue until one or the other protagonist is
reduced to helplessness. When this occurs between individuals or
small groups, the consequences are bad enough. When it happens
between nations, the results can be catastrophic.

Rallying to self-defense is a necessary technique for survival of
the species. It also creates a dilemma for leaders. Effective leadership
requires helping people to change themselves and their belief systems,
not helping them hold to a rigid self-defense. How then can leaders
challenge people's belief systems without threatening them?

Threat and Tunnel Vision

Tunnel vision is the second consequence of threat. When people feel threatened, their perception is narrowed to the threatening object so that other events around them are obscured. The experience is much like looking through a tunnel, and it is familiar to anyone who has been in a car accident and afterward said, "All I could see was that big truck coming at me!" Or perhaps you've been worried about something, and your attention returns to that something over and over despite all efforts to forget it. Extremely pleasant events also may produce tunnel vision. Witness the child's preoccupation with Christmas the closer it approaches. Lovers caught up in the ecstasy of sex are notoriously oblivious to what goes on around them.

Like self-defense, tunnel vision has crucial survival value for humans, but it creates problems for leaders. Tunnel vision restricts attention to the source of threat. Yet bringing about learning and change in people requires broadening experience, not narrowing it. Leaders need to free people, not control them.

The negative aspects of threat somehow must be prevented or circumvented in the processes of effective teaching and leadership. That is sometimes difficult to accomplish when teachers or leaders are perceived by those they work with as authority figures. People with the power to affect our welfare can be threatening simply by the nature of the positions they hold. Unless leaders are aware of how things seem to coworkers or students, their efforts can be severely undermined. The conscientious practice of empathy as discussed in Chapter 2 is an important skill for navigating these potential minefields.

Learning and Change

The purpose of educational leadership is to facilitate learning and change to successfully achieve the goals of education. From the behavioral view of human behavior, that calls for manipulation of the forces exerted on people to assure their arrival at the intended goals. Many of today's leaders know no other way to influence learning and change. Yet as we observed in Chapter 1, this behavioral approach has serious flaws and cannot be counted on. A person-centered viewpoint requires something entirely different. If the causes of behavior lie in the individual's belief systems, it follows that real learning or change must be a consequence of helping people modify their perceptions or beliefs.

In 1949, Snygg and Combs stated that any information will affect a person's behavior only in the degree to which the person has discovered its personal meaning (Combs, 1982). To illustrate this principle, we might think of all information on a continuum, as in Figure 3.1. At one end is information that seems to have no relationship to a person; at the other end are information and events perceived as deeply meaningful.

Using the chart in Figure 3.1, let us suppose that Jan Smith is reading a newspaper. She scans the local hospital statistics. In the list of conditions treated, her eyes skim over the notation, "Huntington's Chorea, 4 cases."

Figure 3.1. Continuum of Relationship to Self

Not self						Self
A	B	C	D	E	F	G

On the continuum at point **A:** Jan hasn't the slightest idea what Huntington's Chorea is, but the concept has entered her awareness. The information has no effect on her behavior, and it goes "in one ear and out the other." Later that week the term is mentioned by one of Jan's friends during a conversation.

B: Jan recognizes it as a term she is unfamiliar with, and later in the day she looks it up. She finds the term applies to a hereditary disease that begins in adulthood and is characterized by choreic movements and mental deterioration. Onset is insidious. Symptoms usually begin between ages 30 and 50. They involve personality changes and a host of other unpleasant conditions. Jan now "knows" the concept intellectually.

C: The concept still has almost no effect on Jan's behavior. Let us suppose now that Jan hears about a fellow employee over in the shipping department who has just learned she has Huntington's Chorea.

D: Now the term has more personal meaning for Jan. The disease is happening to a fellow worker. Jan now feels a vague uneasiness about the disorder and talks about it with colleagues in product development where she works. A few days later, Sally Brown, Jan's golf partner, tells Jan she has just heard from her doctor that she has this disease.

E: Jan is horrified at what is happening to her friend. She listens, offers support and encouragement, thinks about the matter frequently, and discusses it with many other people.

F: Imagine next the effect on Jan's life and behavior when she hears that her elderly parent has it.

G: Or imagine when Jan finds out that she has the disease herself! Obviously, the greater the personal meaning, the greater the effect on behavior. Learning, changing beliefs, or changing behavior really is a problem in changing personal meaning.

The Discovery of Personal Meaning

Learning has two facets: (1) confronting an experience and (2) discovering what it means to the self. Most of us are experts at the first part. We know how to give and get information. In today's world, we also have marvelous machines capable of providing information in greater quantities, in more dramatic fashion, and more rapidly than ever before. As a matter of fact, these machines can provide information far more effectively than teachers. These machines could have made teachers as fountainheads of knowledge obsolete if there were no other reasons for employment of teachers. There is a vast difference, however, between knowing and behaving, between mere knowledge and giving personal meaning to the knowledge.

Many people, including teachers and educational leaders, operate under the false assumption that people are not learning anything unless they are being subjected to more information. As a matter of fact, information overload can stop the learning process altogether. Many important learnings occur without any new information whatever. Take the concept of the Golden Rule: "Do unto others as you would have them do unto you." Few of us need more information about this age-old maxim. What is needed is time and opportunity to explore the deeper and deeper personal meaning of the thought. The key to truly effective learning or change lies not in providing more information but in guiding people to the discovery of personal meaning about the information.

Learners must actively participate in the personal discovery of meaning. This process also takes time. Many a promising attempt at learning or behavior change has been aborted because teachers or leaders were in a rush. Giving an order, making a demand, or providing information too rapidly can sidetrack or distort the processes of discovering meaning, which are essential for learning or behavior change.

Feeling and Emotion in Learning and Change

It is widely believed that learning is a logical, objective matter in which there is little room for human qualities like feeling and emotion. That assumption is a fallacy. Effective learning is a deeply personal matter. The more deeply personal a perception, the more likely it is to be accompanied by feelings and emotions. We do not feel emotional about matters of no importance to us.

Emotion is part of our survival instincts. When our ancestors walked the forest trail and came face to face with a bear, they needed an extra shot of strength to fight or flee the scene. Nature has provided that emergency boost in the physiological concomitant of emotion, which we experience as "feelings."

Earlier we observed how Jan Smith's behavior was affected by her learning about Huntington's Chorea. The more personal meaning this nasty disease posed for her, the greater was her emotional response. Reading statistics about the condition or looking it up produced very little change in her behavior, nor did it result in much feeling. As experience with the disease came closer to herself, her behavior became more marked, and so did her emotion and feeling. The closer events are perceived to the self, the greater the feeling and emotion.

Many educational observers believe that there is no room for feeling and emotion in public schools. They complain that these human reactions interfere with effective learning. There are even teachers and administrators who endorse this view. Yet if learning and change are functions of the deeper and deeper discovery of personal meaning, and if feeling and emotion are concomitant to personal meaning, the lack of feeling and emotion in a classroom, school, or program must signify that little real learning is happening there. The presence of feeling is an indicator of the degree to which learning is occurring. People don't feel much about things of little importance to them. They feel a great deal about matters of personal significance.

Feelings are our shorthand ways of trying to convey the nature of our extremely complex personal meanings at any moment. Personal meanings have to do with our beliefs, attitudes, hopes, wants, and desires. They also may include knowledge and previous experience, the situation confronted, and the state of the physical body, to name but a few of the many factors involved. All this is much too complex to be expressed simply to someone else. Accordingly, we report our complex personal meanings as "feelings."

For example, we use words like *angry, touched, afraid, anxious, attracted to,* or *repelled by.* Yet those simple words express only a small sample of the personal meanings being experienced. They are never totally adequate to express the full nature of our personal experience.

Lovers throughout history have complained about the inadequacy of "I love you" to convey all they want to express. Nevertheless, feelings are indicators of our belief systems. As such, they are far more important in understanding ourselves or other people than the knowledge we possess or the objective ideas they express. It is human feelings that hold the keys to understanding ourselves or anyone else.

These ideas hold many implications for educational leaders. Leaders often are inundated with "things" problems, and their job responsibilities require immediate action or decision. Responding to such demands can lead the leader into a mindset where problem solving becomes the main job description. Then, concentration on things quickly becomes so demanding that it robs the leader of time to consider what is truly important. It also can frustrate colleagues and coworkers who find their leader caught up in a web of "administrivia." The leader's work becomes essentially reactive, responding to events rather than facilitating innovation and the healthy development of programs and personnel.

Learning and Communication

The conception of learning outlined above is linked to important understandings about communication. Communication occurs when the perceptions of a speaker (or writer, lecturer, or boss) find counterparts in the perceptions of the hearer (or receiver, student, or audience). How well people communicate is thus a function of the overlap of their perceptions. The same principles governing learning apply as well to communication. Any information will be understood by the receiver only in the degree to which he or she has discovered its personal meaning. Until information is incorporated into the belief system of the receiver, nothing has truly occurred.

It is not enough simply to give people information. When we do not get an expected response to something we've tried to communicate, it's all too easy to say, "Can't she see?" or "Well, I told him what to do!" or "Honestly, they simply don't listen!" or "I can't help it if she's too stupid to understand." To be sure, leaders are expected to listen to their teachers, and teachers need to listen to their principals or supervisors. That is expected as part of their roles. But listening does not guarantee understanding. Understanding comes with the personal discovery of meaning, an event teachers or educational leaders do not control. If people do not understand what we want to convey, the fault lies not with them but in ourselves.

Our own beliefs always have the feeling of reality. The important concepts in our belief system are usually the final products of personal discovery, often formed over a considerable period of time or as a consequence of much experience. Rarely is it possible, therefore, to communicate deep personal meanings to others simply or directly. It will take time and sustained effort for our own personal meanings to become important in someone else's belief system.

Educational leaders, like others in a things-oriented culture, have been deeply ingrained in the manipulation-of-forces approach to events. Operating on that assumption about how people change, it seems only natural to tell, order, demonstrate, show, or write when we wish to communicate with others. Unfortunately, as we have seen, effective learning always has two parts: new information and discovering its meaning. All the communication techniques in the previous list deal with only the first of those factors. Giving information cannot be counted on to communicate with others without their involvement in the discovery of personal meaning. "Telling" is a vastly overrated device for communication. So is "teaching," if teachers do no more than lecture or instruct. Experienced lecturers, for example, know that an audience rarely can absorb more than two or three points from a single speech. Accordingly, speakers use repetition, illustration, anecdotes, and drama to help their audiences begin the process of personal discovery of meaning.

There are no infallible methods to assure communication. Understanding that communication does not occur until the receiver has discovered its personal meaning, however, can help educational leaders avoid the error of thinking their task is done on delivery of the message. One major reason for the failures of educational reform over the past 50 years is the attempt to bring about change by administrative, top-down fiat. Teachers cannot be expected to carry out mandates they do not comprehend or agree with.

Any consideration of communication must recognize that what is communicated is not just the words of the intended message. People gain personal meanings from the experience of the effort. Communication is affected deeply by the place where it occurs, the demeanor of the communicator, and the feelings people have about him or her, not just now but also from previous experience.

Effective communication is more than a simple matter of style or method. It is a complex matter of facilitating the discovery of personal meaning for the receiver. How well educational leaders accomplish that end depends on their awareness of the meanings colleagues hold and their own belief systems, goals, and ways of behaving.

The Importance of Self-Concept

What people believe about themselves is vital to every aspect of human behavior. We have seen how it plays a major role in the nature of human need and motivation and its role in challenge and threat, communication, learning and change. Anything that important in human behavior must, of necessity, be a vital factor for educational leadership. Understanding the self-concepts of others is of crucial importance to leaders as they assess their coworkers, plan professional strategies, interact and communicate, or facilitate learning and change in students and teachers. How leaders affect the self-concepts of those around them will determine in large measure the leaders' success or failure.

The crucial character of people's self-concepts emphasizes a leader's need for empathy. Low levels of teacher self-concept are practically endemic in public schools. Low public regard, the nature and structure of school organization, treatment of teachers as "delivery systems," overwork, and underpay have seriously undermined the self-concepts of large numbers of teachers. This has resulted in widespread "burnout." Too often, such negative feelings about self are exacerbated by philosophies of management and control.

Whatever leaders do in interacting with others must begin from the most accurate understanding of how people see themselves, the situations they are in, and the purposes they seek to fulfill. Self-concepts are not changed by telling people what to believe. They are formed from human experience. People learn who and what they are through the personal meanings acquired from the things or events that happen to them. It follows that whatever leaders do must be assessed in terms of the personal meanings their actions have on those they serve.

Effective Feedback

If learning and change are understood as the personal discovery of meaning, it follows that learners need to be continuously aware of where they are and where they need to go. This calls for some kind of knowledge of results, or feedback. But what should this feedback be like? From the principles of learning stated above, we can list several criteria for providing feedback that stimulates and encourages learning and change. Though these criteria apply to motivation everywhere, they are especially relevant for education. For example, current grading systems in U.S. public schools don't fulfill any of the following elements.

1. Feedback should be immediate. For maximal learning, feedback or evaluation should occur as soon after an event as possible. Learning is directly affected by the perceived relationship to the self. The closer the event to the self, the more powerful the motivating effect.

2. Feedback should be personal. Learners need to know continuously where they are and what needs to be done next. This is a highly personal type of data, quite unrelated to what others may be doing. Comparing one learner to another contributes nothing at all to comprehension of what the learners just did or what they need to do next. Comparison with others simply labels learners, and labels do very little to encourage discovery of personal meaning. Instead, labels divert attention from the task at hand to the learner's standing as a competitor. Whatever distracts a learner from the discovery of personal meaning is just a roadblock to true learning.

3. Feedback should be challenging, not threatening. People feel challenged by tasks that interest them and that they believe they can handle; they feel threatened by tasks that they don't believe they can achieve. Threatening feedback focuses attention on the source of threat rather than the feedback information.

4. Feedback should be relevant to the task. Feedback should focus attention on the task itself, and satisfaction should be in the accomplishment. A wise teacher once chided another for using comments like "That's good, Helen!" or "I like that, Ned!" as motivation for students. The teacher explained, "When you say things like that, it puts the locus of satisfaction in pleasing you. You need to keep the satisfaction in the task itself or its outcomes." Learning for some extraneous or artificially contrived reward or punishment distracts the learner from the main task, and it is likely to result in temporary or distorted learning.

5. Feedback should point the way to next steps. If possible, effective feedback should do more than simply report progress. Motivation is greatly enhanced if the feedback helps the learner perceive what comes next. Feedback is most effective when it offers clues to the next steps, suggests hypotheses to be explored, or points to mistakes that can be corrected.

Many educational leaders are required, as part of their jobs, to evaluate people they work with or supervise. From a person-centered orientation, the processes of evaluation are much more than arriving at an objective rating of individuals and their performance. Educational leaders should consider how the preceding criteria affect evaluation. And if they are at all concerned about how evaluations affect people and their performance, leaders will have to consider such person-centered factors as personal need, challenge and threat, personal meaning, self-concept, and motivation.

The Nature of a Healthy Personality

Person-centered thinking maintains that our basic drive is toward health and the maintenance and enhancement of self. But what is the nature of health? For many years, health was regarded in physical terms, as "being well" or "not sick." To psychologists it was a matter of being "nondeviant," a question of a person's position on the "normal curve" into which human traits seem to fall. That conception of health has never been satisfactory to educators. It equates health with being in the middle of the curve. But who, after all, wants to be average? More recently, professionals have looked at health in terms of ultimate goals. In medicine, researchers seek the nature of "high-level wellness," and perceptual psychologists explore "self-actualization" or "self-fulfillment."

There are two ways to examine the question of self-actualization. You can approach it externally to ask, "What are the traits or characteristics of self-actualizers?" From this view we arrive at characteristics such as openness to experience, an unhostile sense of humor, autonomy, problem centering, clear discrimination between means and ends, creativity, and many more. Listing the traits of self-actualizers in this way is helpful but is essentially descriptive. It tells us what such people are like but provides little help in understanding the dynamics of how they got that way or how to help others achieve such traits.

Examining self-actualization from a person-centered perspective, investigators have studied healthy humans from an internal frame of reference, trying to understand them from their own viewpoint. Examined in that way, self-actualizing people seem to have four major characteristics: they are well informed, they see themselves in positive ways, they are accepting of themselves and their worlds, and they have deep feelings of oneness or identification with others (Combs, 1962a).

Knowledge

To function even passively in our complex technological society requires a great deal of knowledge. Self-actualizers are more well informed than most. This is not to say they have advanced college degrees, however. Self-actualizers don't necessarily possess academic knowledge; rather, they possess the knowledge they need to function well with the people and settings with whom and in which they live and work.

Positive View of Self

Highly self-actualized people possess positive views of self. They see themselves as liked, wanted, acceptable, and able citizens of dignity and integrity. Such feelings carry great advantages. Positive views of self provide a secure and stable base from which to launch excursions into the world. Seeing themselves as such, people can afford to take risks. Thus, they are more likely to be creative and innovative. Feeling positive about themselves, people deal with life straightforwardly and authentically instead of fearfully and tentatively. A positive sense of self is an enormous resource.

Acceptance of Reality

Self-actualizing people have a high capacity to confront the world as they encounter it and to enter into effective and satisfying relationships with it. They deal with the world accurately, realistically, and with a minimum of distortion. This is sometimes called "acceptance," being able to confront what is. It should not be confused with resignation, giving up, or being cynical. Self-actualizing people confront themselves and the world, including negative events and unpleasantness, straightforwardly. Positive feelings about themselves make it possible for them to accept themselves and the world without distortion or denial.

Feelings of Oneness or Identification

Self-actualizing people have deep feelings of oneness or identification with others. They have a feeling of continuity with humanity, a sense of oneness in the human condition. Such feelings make it possible for them to enter into human relationships much more openly and deeply. Feelings of identification are immensely facilitating to almost any human relationship. Self-actualizers enter relationships expecting to be accepted and cared about and, hence, are more likely to have their expectation fulfilled.

The production of healthy, self-actualizing people is a fundamental purpose of education. Its achievement is more likely if leaders themselves approach self-actualization. People with the above qualities are valuable to any group whether as leaders, teachers, friends, marital partners, or citizens.

୧୧ ୧୧ ୧୧

Effective leaders are true professionals. Their task is much more than the simple application of tools or procedures to the problems of education. Professionals are not machines. They are thinking, problem-solving people. They bring to their tasks belief systems acquired from knowledge and experience. With this framework, they confront the problems of the profession and use themselves to bring about effective solutions. This creative process involves their own belief systems and the belief systems of those with whom they interact.

In Chapters 1 and 3, we have outlined some of the basic principles concerning human behavior, growth, and change established in modern person-centered thinking. These concepts have enormous implications for all aspects of education. They are particularly significant for educational leadership. They affect how leaders set their goals, carry out their tasks, interact with colleagues, even what they believe about educational leadership itself. In the next chapters we elaborate on these basic principles of human growth and development and apply the principles specifically to person-centered school leaders.

CREATING AN ENVIRONMENT FOR LEARNING AND CHANGE

TRADITIONALLY, SCHOOL CULTURES DO NOT VALUE AND ADDRESS people's needs. Most school cultures do not even expect or encourage strong feelings and emotions—or even passion. They don't create environments where people communicate honestly and helpfully, where competition takes a back seat to collaboration. In fact, quite the opposite usually is true.

Yet as we discussed in Chapter 3, learning and change occur in an environment where

- learners' needs are understood, appreciated, and attended to;
- people are challenged to grow and change, not threatened to change;
- learning is accompanied by strong feeling and emotion;
- communication and feedback are frequent, are relevant, and suggest next steps; and
- collaboration, not competition, characterizes learning activities.

If these assumptions about learning and change are true—and we believe they are—school leaders face several challenges in creating schools where learning is not only possible but is encouraged and nurtured. For the remainder of this chapter, we will explore school culture and how it enhances or detracts from learning and change.

Learning and Need

Rarely are people's true needs discussed in schools. Sometimes, creating a learning environment to address people's true needs is corrupted by individuals competing to fulfill their own needs for power, status, protection, and autonomy. Other times, true needs are lost amidst a hundred other "needs."

- Faculty and staff discuss the *need* to cover material. But why not look at everyone's need—not just students'—to understand basic concepts, practice skills, apply new information to different contexts, and integrate new understanding?
- Many see a *need* for higher scores on mandated achievement tests or the *need* to improve ACT and SAT scores. What if they instead considered all students' needs for seeing that their efforts are significant and meaningful? What if they considered all students' needs for knowing that their work will lead to appropriate recognition or reward?
- Many schools see a *need* to win athletic, drama, music, or art contests. Instead of enhancing the image of an individual school through contests, or enhancing individuals by putting them in competitive situations to "win," schools could address people's needs to participate in challenging events with others to learn how to perform at peak levels.
- Teachers and administrators discuss the *need* to "get our grades done." Could they not address the need for everyone to communicate "how we are doing"?

- Sometimes, schools see a *need* to "get rid of kids" who do not conform to rules, or the *need* to "get rid of teachers" who don't conform to rules. Instead, schools could look at everyone's need to stake out a place in the organization where he or she belongs and to find identity in various activities within the school community.
- Some see a *need* to hide deficiencies from the school board, or a *need* to protect the school and its employees from outside observers. Individuals say they *need* to protect themselves from critics, and some teachers say they *need* to be left alone to teach "whatever I want to teach." But instead of focusing on a need for protection, we could look at the need for everyone to understand and respect the effort that schooling requires along with the complexity that confronts every person who tries to work well in the school system.
- Many see a *need* to be absolved of accountability for performance, or a *need* to have individual rights protected before the rights of others. Instead of looking at the need to be absolved of accountability, schools, and especially their critics, could look at human beings' needs to have their efforts recognized for what they are: good faith attempts to do their best. They also would consider the need to be free from fear of failing and fear of letting down people for whom they willingly have accepted responsibility.

How Needs Affect the Organization

It is important for school leaders to see needs as they are, not as they are presented through outward behavior. Sometimes this new vision requires leaders to strip away people's layers of pretense and get down to the basics of why and how they want to organize themselves within the school community. If schools are to nurture learning and change, organizations of people—including students, teachers, parents, administrators, custodians, and secretaries—must allow everyone to grow without fear of being ridiculed or demeaned for expressing needs.

This stripping-down process is tricky. People hide their needs from each other for many reasons. Usually this includes fear, embarrassment, inadequacy, mistrust, anger, and frustration. When leaders ask people to be more open, honest, and truthful about their needs, they must be prepared to handle the strong emotions that emerge when people discover that the environment is safe to do just that. This process can be painful and confrontational. It also allows some to abuse the openness that is a prerequisite for truthfulness. People can be hurt by openness and retreat into defensiveness, or they will withdraw from participating at all. Many times, the school leader becomes the lightning rod for all the pent-up resentment and hostility that hasn't been addressed. This type of situation may call for external assistance as staff members begin to work through the conflict in the school, conflict brought on by unmet needs.

Leaders may wonder if all of this attention to *need* is worth the pain. Senge (1990) addresses this issue when he says:

> Organizations learn only through individuals who learn. Individual learning does not guarantee organizational learning. But without it, no organizational learning occurs (p. 139).

If individuals are to learn, that learning must address their needs. Ignoring needs creates an environment where the organization stagnates and dies; it does not become vibrant and dynamic, growing and changing as individuals grow and change.

Leaders often encounter "the ghost of Christmas past" as they try to unravel what everyone needs and wants from daily existence at the school. These ghosts haunt the school in many ways. They are the evil spirits of all the horrible things that people perceive happened before the leader came (or even after he or she came). It may be something as simple as a kindergarten teacher who scolded a child unfairly or something as complicated as an entire program of studies that was written by the faculty and turned down by an administrator "in charge."

People remember these kinds of things for a long time, and many issues haunt discussions long after they should have been buried with a proper funeral. Out of sheer frustration, leaders often are tempted just to tell people to "get a life" and forget the past. Unfortunately, that response never makes the "ghosts" go away. It simply locks the events even longer into people's memories as they decide this new leader is just one more person who "doesn't understand."

These ghosts represent a bitterness that never sweetens with time, and they are an important part of the culture of any school. Unfortunately, they block the process of change and growth in the organization the same way that inaccurate facts from past learning and thoughtless, unchallenged ideas block academic understanding and growth.

Leaders who want to get anywhere in the process of creating an environment for learning and change cannot forget to address people's needs, including their own. These needs vary considerably, but they affect the behavior of every individual who interacts with the school.

Students' Needs for Achievement and Recognition

Earlier in this chapter we mentioned test scores, grades, and contests as vehicles by which students, teachers, and parents get information about student achievement. Although we know that most school boards and states would not consider dropping required achievement tests, especially in an era of increased interest in "standards," it does seem possible that the dialogue could be broadened to include an understanding of students' needs for achievement and how schools might meet them.

The Need for Meaning

With tests driving curriculum, teachers might be lulled into believing that their mission is to help kids do well on achievement tests and on aptitude tests like the ACT and SAT. To accomplish this mission, they begin to see their role as "covering material." Lesson plans take on a meaning all their own as teachers worry about familiarizing students with enough content.

School board members and parents want high test scores. Administrators are held accountable for their schools' scores even though they have no control over how well kids do. Faculty members get printouts of how students in their classrooms perform compared to students in other classrooms. Teachers begin to see that they are compared with other teachers based on how well the children in their classes perform. The numbers game begins to drive everyone's efforts, sometimes to the detriment of real learning and growth.

Achievement tests give one picture of the growth that children experience in a school, but it is, after all, only one picture. Children and adolescents need to grasp basic concepts that are the foundation of learning. To understand new concepts, students need opportunities to practice the new skills and knowledge they are learning about, opportunities to apply them to a variety of contexts, and opportunities to integrate old knowledge and skills into new knowledge and skills. "Covering material" doesn't fit well into this scheme of learning. Instead, it hints of dissemination of information and lots of "stuff" being crammed into students' heads so they can repeat the "stuff" on a test. This kind of knowledge is quickly forgotten. Interacting with information is what enhances learning and growth.

The following activities disseminate information: reading about poverty, seeing a movie about poverty, learning statistics about poverty. But what about students' needs to make meaning of this information, to apply it to their lives, to sense that they have engaged in something significant and important, and to know that they have performed well at understanding new knowledge? These needs are not met through books, articles, movies, or statistics. Instead, they are met by working in the fields with migrant workers, donating tutoring hours to the local community center, collecting used clothing for a thrift shop, gathering canned food to stock the county's food shelf, building a house with Habitat for Humanity, taking up a collection to buy athletic shoes for kids who otherwise couldn't afford to play on sports teams, going to the grocery store for elderly shut-ins, distributing food through Meals on Wheels, cooking for a homeless shelter, providing free baby-sitting for young kids so that parents can have an evening out with little cost, fund raising for scholarship money for school activities, being a Big Brother or Big Sister, or sending school supplies to students in other countries who have no materials.

The list of these kinds of activities is endless, and each fulfills students' needs to engage in learning that changes their perspectives, knowledge, meanings, and understandings. These kinds of activities allow students to connect meaningfully with others to do important things, and they could be normal events built into every school's life. They offer the chance for students to practice skills, apply information, integrate new knowledge. Teachers' dialogue as they develop a curriculum would best take into consideration students' needs for life-altering experiences. This kind of dialogue is far more important than that which takes place around "covering material."

The Need for Achievement Outside Classrooms

How does a leader respond meaningfully to students' needs to achieve outside the classroom? Contests and awards are pervasive in schools. There are poster contests, essay contests, American Legion citizenship awards, basketball tournaments, debate tournaments, auto repair contests, and drama contests. It seems these competitions are never ending, and they begin to take on lives separate from what the school is all about.

Students enjoy these activities partly because they offer a chance for achievement that differs from achievement in the classroom. First, these contests often are more "real" than classroom activities. There is nothing quite as authentic as Rachel's heave of a basketball from beyond the three-point line that for the first time swishes the net. That feels like true achievement. So does Marcus's sterling performance of the doomed Julius Caesar, or Jill's abstract watercolor hanging at the county art show, or Keith's smile of accomplishment as he finally masters Mozart's clarinet concerto. These authentic challenges can bring out the best in students.

Schools must discover how to make these kinds of activities available to all students and how to instill in each student the idea that participation in the event is the true achievement, not the winning. When we reward only winners, we denigrate the losers. And wherever there are winners, there are many more losers. So contests and awards must be handled carefully. Both individual and team progress must be honored—not winning. We must honor students when they overcome obstacles, conquer fear, face personal inadequacy, suppress individual needs and desires for the good of the team, make efforts to help others be successful, persist in the face of perceived failure, and exhibit humility amidst personal acclaim. Recognizing these achievements leads to greater personal learning and growth. Even those who don't "win" can achieve peak performance when it is judged in these ways.

Person-centered school leaders can make a tremendous positive impact on a school when they attend to students' needs for achievement beyond test scores and winning contests. When individual and team progress, participation, and collaboration are the "standards," students' needs for personal achievement and recognition are met in ways that will produce positive learning, change, and growth. When the journey toward growth becomes the reward in itself, students will know the meaning of achievement in a much different way than numbered scores on tests.

Adults' Needs for Achievement

Faculty and other adults in the school also have needs for achievement and recognition. To create an environment for learning and growth, leaders must recognize and attend to these adult needs. Since adults in the school are vested with the responsibility to create opportunities for student achievement and recognition, it makes common sense that they must deal with their own needs for the same things before they can be of much help to children.

The traditional school culture rewards competition, autonomy, and individualism within a faculty, so the journey toward achievement and recognition is sometimes frustrating for both leaders and teachers. Many teachers don't like being singled out for their achievements in front of others for fear that people will perceive them as arrogant, "stuck on themselves," or "better" than others. This environment is an inevitable result of the competitive and individualistic nature of teaching.

Recognizing Need for Meaning in Adults

Leaders must help teachers and other adults in the school understand the nature of personal mastery and growth and the forces within the school that seem to prevent the celebration of everyone's achievements. How can teachers foster the notion of collaboration and teamwork in students when they don't allow themselves the opportunity to achieve and be recognized through collaboration? As with students, the things we select to recognize and celebrate as high achievement among the faculty are not necessarily the things that capture people's sense of meaning and purpose.

It is important to spend time considering what is important to recognize. The shared vision and purpose that drive the school should hint at what those important things are. For example, these kinds of achievement make faculty and staff members' work something to celebrate: helping students grow, reflecting on personal and professional growth, asking penetrating and challenging questions, guarding the collective conscience of the organization, helping incorporate parents meaningfully into the ongoing dialogue of the school, and developing programs or courses of study that allow students to expand their knowledge and meaning in ways the school had not thought of before. Recognizing these kinds of achievements captures people's imagination and hearts rather than just their heads and hands.

Adult Needs Outside Classrooms

Adults also have needs to be recognized as fully functioning people with hopes and dreams that go beyond their classroom doors. Leaders can go a long way toward developing a learning environment at school if they know the kinds of experiences adults are having outside of school that are causing them to grow and change. These experiences certainly have an impact on the learning that occurs at school, and sometimes they even get in the way of adults learning "on the job."

Acknowledging these kinds of needs and experiences means that school leaders recognize teachers and staff members as real people with real lives. It also means recognizing that learning occurs in a variety of settings, with adults as well as with students. When leaders listen to the faculty and staff and hear their personal stories of challenge and mastery, they model a true learning environment that takes into account all the things that are going on with people, things that either hinder or nurture growth.

School leaders don't have to develop contrived methods for this recognition. Just visiting with faculty and staff on a regular basis to find out what they are doing and thinking about—and then following up with that knowledge—is sometimes enough. Formal and informal rituals help, too, but these rituals should be thoughtful, not just something that people carry out for the sake of carrying them out. Here is an appealing example of a staff ritual:

> A school in Beaverton, Oregon, has developed a ritual of an end-of-the-year storytelling session. Any person can tell a story and compete in the "Berries and Pits" contest. A prize is given to the person who tells the best "berry" story and the best "pit" story. This ritual gives people an opportunity to celebrate hideous failures, so hideous that they have become comical. They also honor heartwarming successes.

The stories go a long way toward building community and developing a sense of what is important and what is not. They also offer a chance to good-naturedly acknowledge human foibles and triumphs in a collaborative, celebratory environment. Applause determines the winners. The principal then gives out the awards, small tokens that are clever and funny. Everyone leaves school for the summer with a reaffirmation of what it means to be an adult in that school building: helping kids learn and grow. The adults also are recognized as learners themselves.

Challenge Versus Threat

Threat is one of the primary forces that stifles learning. People with authority, influence, or personal power can coerce others into doing things by using threat to instill fear: of failure, of breaking a rule, of facing ridicule or humiliation, of personal inadequacy.

Threat is one of the most commonly used motivators in schools. Teachers threaten students with poor marks, loss of recess, calls to parents, discipline by the principal, detention, social isolation, humiliation, and more verbal abuse either through criticism or sarcasm. Principals threaten teachers with poor performance ratings, constant surveillance, assignment to undesirable teaching positions, even the loss of their jobs if they don't perform to externally mandated standards. Superintendents threaten principals with poor performance ratings if their schools don't meet district standards or if parents complain too much or if student behavior seems less than appropriate.

The problem with using the threat of punishment to improve learning and teaching is that it either paralyzes or angers people. People who feel threatened withdraw from others, withhold information, become defensive, rationalize themselves out of responsibilities, or act out their anger by becoming hostile and negative. People who feel threatened are afraid, refuse to take risks, won't try new skills, don't practice things they don't know well, avoid trying new methods, sidestep exploring strange and unusual ideas, and balk at seeking new associations and meaning. Instead, they retreat into ways of doing and thinking that are comfortable; they will not challenge directly the person who can dole out the punishment or make the threat stick. They search for ways to not be noticed, to stay the course, to maintain the status quo, or to sabotage the leader's efforts.

Learning cannot flourish in such a climate. For learning to occur, people must be able to experience new thoughts and ideas, work them into some new schema that makes sense to them, and then construct some kind of new personal meaning from the experience. If people are threatened, their energies will be devoted to defending how they are, or how they are thinking, rather than trying on new ways of thinking. People who perceive threat will not move forward with new ideas and new methods, and they will not risk trying new experiences. Therefore, their ability to learn will be stifled. They will stay stuck in old ways until they feel safe enough to try out new ones.

Threat is also perceived when people believe that the tasks they are asked to do seem too difficult to accomplish. They believe that if they try them, they will fail. They are fearful because they do not believe they have the necessary skills and knowledge to accomplish the expected tasks at a level that is proficient. So they duck out of them if they can, or rationalize some reason why they don't have to do them, or pretend some kind of success that never really happened, thereby shutting themselves out of any learning.

In the following example, faculty members perceived that kind of threat occurred:

> A high school was attempting to initiate a new self-directed learning block for students. A task force of teachers, students, and the principal talked for some time about the curriculum and the schedule. When the principal asked students and teachers, "Where in the curriculum do students have opportunities to practice becoming lifelong, self-directed learners?" no one could think of a place, even though the development of lifelong, self-directed learners was a stated goal of the

school. From this acknowledged gap came the idea of having time during the school day where students would be responsible for their own learning, assisted by a teacher who would help them plan their project.

This all seemed like a good idea. A professor from the local university volunteered to teach a two-semester course in autonomous learning to teachers who were interested. A self-directed learning task force was created to be the advisory group for the change. A pilot class was developed and implemented. Parents and students were educated about the new direction. Parents served on the advisory group, and students and teachers got ready to start.

Two years after its initiation, the program was gone. Why? There were a variety of reasons. One of the main reasons, however, was because the change required faculty to reconceive their entire way of relating to students. This change was so enormous that it seemed overwhelmingly threatening. The principal did not anticipate the depth of this threat. To her the change was an interesting challenge; to many teachers, however, it was a threat, and not an interesting one at that. Many of them responded by avoiding the program, criticizing it, rationalizing why it was not needed, pretending success that was not really there, bad-mouthing it, suggesting that the principal had been out of the classroom too long, complaining that they did not have enough support from the principal. Never once did the faculty and principal have an honest, open dialogue about the strengths and weaknesses of the innovation, even though the program was wildly successful with some students, a miserable failure with others, and perceived around the state as an innovative way to restructure the school day so students could practice self-direction of their own learning. The change was too big a threat to the faculty who had to carry out the program.

Why was this program a threat rather than a challenge? Perhaps the task seemed too hard to be accomplished with the proficiency that the faculty demanded of themselves. The leader did not see in advance that more preparation, discussion, and ownership were needed before the innovation could be explored and carried out successfully.

Turning Threat into Challenge

One odd thing about threat is that it doesn't even have to be real to be perceived. Some people perceive threat where there is none. Nervous students who want to please the adults in their lives or who are afraid of failing can perceive situations as threatening even when the teacher has done a good job of building a nurturing climate. These students need care and encouragement and lots of strong messages telling them that they are just fine the way they are. Without this care they will be unable to engage in joyful learning.

Some teachers, too, live out their unresolved authority issues with their principals. No matter how encouraging or nurturing the school leader is, these teachers perceive threat in the principal's every act and every question. They hide their true feelings, disguise their classroom troubles, seek sympathy from their colleagues by complaining about the thoughtless leadership of the school, and resist or sabotage any effort or change that might reveal how they truly perform or believe.

These teachers present a serious challenge to the school leadership. To hold them to standards can appear threatening, and they almost always respond by being overly defensive or critical of the person who asks questions. It can be helpful to enlist the assistance of other teachers in working with these insecure educators to build their skills and, therefore, their self-confidence. Sometimes a strong teacher mentor can be the best help if the fear of evaluation and judgment is vested in the principal. Staff development activities built around a performance improvement plan also can help by allowing the teacher to get out of the school setting into a neutral place to learn new skills.

Although threat can stifle a learning environment, so can a lack of challenge. The dilemma of creating a learning environment is in finding activities and experiences for students and teachers alike that are challenging enough to cause them to learn yet not so difficult that they are perceived as threats. People must be challenged to reach personal mastery. If the only experiences available to them are too easy, they will become bored and indifferent, and they will lose the motivation to learn and push themselves toward higher performance and knowledge. Their motivation still will be high, since humans always are motivated toward some kind of action, but it won't be toward reaching the goal of the school to become a learning environment. Their motivation even may become the disruption of the entire process of schooling!

It is not easy to create a learning environment where external obstacles are seen as challenges, not threats, and where internal creation of tension is challenging, not threatening. Leaders have to search for gaps between the vision of the school and people's behavior, gaps between the vision of the school and its policies and procedures. Once these gaps are identified, the leader can facilitate dialogue about these gaps so people come to see them as challenges that encourage growth, not threats.

Feeling and Emotion

The process of school is fraught with difficulties and dilemmas, mostly because the events and activities of the day affect people's lives dramatically. Doing well at school assures students the opportunity for future success. Doing well at school tends to get translated as getting good grades, both in academics and in character, as judged by adults. Getting good grades tends to get translated into being a "good" and "capable" person. Conversely, getting bad grades tends to get translated into being a "bad" and "incapable" person. It should be no surprise that emotions and feelings run high in students who attend school. The stakes are high—very high. Each day, every student is being judged—and being judged as good or bad, capable or incapable, worthy or unworthy. That kind of judgment is serious business, and it's very difficult to cope with if you happen to be a person who is judged as wanting intellectually or morally.

This kind of emotion and feeling is not what we are talking about when we say emotion and feeling must be present to create an environment for learning and change. The kinds of emotion and feelings that emanate from being judged are brought on by fear and threat. They stifle learning and creativity. They lead to anxiety, fear of failure, lack of risk taking, and defensiveness. All of those emotions suppress the opportunity to learn.

The kinds of emotion and feelings that *are* necessary for optimum learning and growth emanate from the joy of discovery of personal meaning. These emotions guarantee that students and adults alike will pay attention to the learning. They will interact with the content to learn more, to challenge their old assumptions, to grow intellectually by making new associations and connections, and to discard ideas that no longer make sense. This kind of learning captures a person's imagination and heart; this type of learning transforms a learner.

To build a place for true learning, leaders must help enhance the feelings, emotions, and imaginations of learners, both young and old. This kind of school will be noisy and chaotic, cranky and incorrigible, joyous and agreeable, quiet and touching, inviting and inspirational, serious and funny. But it will *never* be passive or exclusive. All learners will be welcomed with open arms and expected to *engage*. All human emotion will be accepted in this place of learning. Everyone will invite, foster, and prompt feelings for events, activities, books, experiences, speakers, music, trips, visitors, and friends. Learners are not learners until they have reorganized their personal meaning systems, and students and adults alike will be asked to do just that: to talk, write, perform, build, create, sing, dance, paint, play, challenge, love, embrace, and discard. All the while they will recognize that this endeavor they are participating in is life-altering. If it isn't, then why bother?

A Reality Check

Does the preceding description fit many schools? No. There is a grimness about schools and their classrooms that is daunting to most learners. Students learn quickly how to adjust their expectations about learning to fit the places we call schools. A researcher enters a kindergarten class and asks the children, "How many of you can sing?" Everyone shoots a hand in the air. She asks, "How many of you can dance?" Everyone shoots a hand in the air. She asks, "How many of you can draw and paint?" Again, all hands go up. By now, the children are all wriggling and squirming in anticipation of telling the researcher how they do those wonderful things.

The same researcher enters a college freshman classroom. She asks, "How many of you can sing?" One hand goes up. She asks, "How many of you can dance?" No hands go up. She asks, "How many of you can draw and paint?" She gets maybe one hand, if she's lucky. So what happened to all of those kindergarten kids who were so skilled at the age of 5 and became so unskilled by the age of 19? They learned to adjust to school. They learned to control their passions, not to follow them. They learned to stifle their feelings and emotions for fear of appearing silly. If they were girls, they also learned not to be too smart, and certainly to be nice and polite and not to have strong opinions. If they were boys, they learned not to cry. They learned to be "strong" and to be angry, frustrated, powerful, and aggressive, but not loving, caring, cooperative, and joyful. And all students learned to be obedient, to follow directions, to do what they were told, to conform, to stay within the lines! They learned these things, that is, if they wanted to be successful at school.

The contrast between what could be cultivated and what actually is cultivated in schools is staggering. There are overwhelming pressures on school leaders to acquiesce to expectations for control, management, authority, rules, policies, and adherence to a dominant culture's values. When leaders try to veer from the "accepted" course, they frequently are forced back "between the lines" by the board of education, superintendent, parents, or even teachers. Sometimes, however, certain circumstances enlighten all of us about the impact of personal construction of meaning through the school curriculum and activities. Consider the following true story.

> The 2nd and 3rd graders in a K–12 school gleaned in the local fields one day. The children were asked to pick all the vegetables left in the fields after the hired workers harvested the crops. It was a hot day, and it was hard work—maybe even a little too hard for 7- and 8-year-olds. But they were plucky souls and collected more than 20,000 pounds of fresh vegetables to donate to the county food shelf, which supplied no-cost food for poor and unemployed people.
>
> At about 4:30, one teacher headed to her car. She saw a small 3rd-grade girl sitting on the cement wall with her mother. The little girl was crying. The teacher walked over to see if she could help. The mother was clearly frustrated and seemed a little annoyed.
>
> The teacher asked, "Stephanie, what's wrong?"
>
> Her mother snapped out a reply: "Can't you see that these kids are just exhausted and were expected to work too hard today? I think this project is just too much for these kids!"
>
> A bit put off by the mother's outburst, the teacher turned back to Stephanie and asked, "Is that what's wrong, Stephanie? Are you just tired?"
>
> She nodded her head and showed how her hands had been rubbed raw. They bled from her work. The teacher hugged her, told her that she had done a good job, and said she'd probably feel a lot better tomorrow. The child sobbed even harder. Perplexed, the teacher bent down and asked quietly, "Is there more that's wrong?"
>
> Stephanie barely nodded her head. The teacher waited. The child cried harder, and her mother looked distraught.
>
> "Do you want to tell me about it, Steph?" the teacher asked. She was beginning to feel a little alarmed.
>
> Stephanie finally said through her tears, "I was thinking about Maria."
>
> "Oh," murmured the teacher. She met the mother's eyes over the child's bent back and lifted her hands in the air to indicate she didn't know any Maria. Then she racked her brain, trying to think of a Maria in Stephanie's class.

"Who is Maria?" the teacher finally asked.

"You don't know her," Stephanie replied. Then she was silent.

"Is Maria crying, too?" the teacher asked, desperately searching her mind for what could possibly be causing such emotion in Stephanie.

"Oh, no, she never cried!" Stephanie exclaimed. "But she wanted to. All the time. And now I know why." Stephanie gained some control over her tears but was still silent.

"Why did she want to cry?" the teacher asked, even more puzzled.

"Because she never got to go to school. All she could do was work in the fields with her mother and father and get her hands all cut up like mine and they bled all the time and she couldn't even put Band-Aids on them to help and she never got to play with any friends or learn to read or anything. We heard all about her yesterday in the movie we saw," said Stephanie.

The teacher was stunned. Stephanie's emotion stemmed from a movie the children had seen in class the day before. It talked about migrant families that worked in the county back in the 1970s. The teacher now remembered signing the purchase order for the movie.

"Well," said the teacher, recovering somewhat. "It sounds like you have learned a lot today about what it would have been like to be Maria, wouldn't you say?"

Stephanie nodded yes.

"What do you think you could do in class tomorrow to help the other kids learn as much as you did?" the teacher asked. Stephanie thought for a minute, then visibly brightened.

"I could do one thing," she said.

"What's that?"

"I could tell them how I cried about my hands bleeding, and I remembered how Maria never cried about hers even though they hurt."

"That sounds like a good idea," the teacher agreed. "Why do you think Maria didn't cry, but you did?" This stumped Stephanie.

"I don't know," she answered finally. "I think I'll ask Mrs. Stuart if I can write about that in my project book and maybe cut out some pictures to go with it."

"Well, that sounds like a good plan for the way to spend your day tomorrow, Stephanie," the teacher replied. The child ran off to get her book bag. Her mother and the teacher just looked at each other in utter amazement.

"I guess I spoke too soon," the mother said.

The teacher replied: "Out of the mouths of babes!"

Feeling and Emotion in Action

The feeling and emotion that Stephanie encountered in the fields that day is at the essence of learning and change. The opportunity for learners to interact with an experience and then to understand how it changes them is what schools can be all about. What can a school leader do to help create that kind of environment?

First, leaders can model strong emotion and passion for the work they do. They can cry when they are moved, laugh when they are delighted, seethe when they are angry, shout when they are frustrated—in short, they can model being human. They can allow all people to express strong feelings and emotions, provided that everyone agrees they must control the actions they take in response to their emotions.

Leaders also can encourage teachers to allow lots of time in classrooms for students to talk about what their experiences mean to them. They can ask teachers to teach students how to process information: to ask questions about what things mean, to ask why they are important, to ask why they should be studied and understood. Leaders also can set expectations that adults in the school will do the same thing when they discuss changes to the school. Leaders can ask teachers questions like: What will it mean to us? How will we change as a result? What will be the impact on others? What will this change mean for our work? How will we explain this to others as something important?

These kinds of questions lead toward shifts in personal construction of meaning. And with these shifts come all the feelings and emotions that accompany new meanings: joy, fear, excitement, anxiety, confidence, uncertainty, sadness, fulfillment. Without the attachment of emotion and feeling to learning, it is doubtful that students and adults will engage in meaningful ways to do the business of school. Instead, they will see learning as a passive, dispassionate endeavor to be completed as soon as possible so that they can get on with the things in their lives that *do* mean something.

One word of caution is in order for leaders beginning to look at ways to bring more authentic human emotion and feeling into school. Expecting and expressing strong emotion and feelings in the learning context is not the usual way of being in school. This new kind of cultural expectation can be threatening to teachers who are not used to being publicly passionate about things. Teachers, too, have learned the ways of school well. They have been rewarded over the years for working dispassionately, for keeping expressions of personal values and beliefs to a minimum, for focusing on results and end products. Teachers or administrators who worry about children's and adults' self-esteem often are labeled "soft" or "nonacademic." Consideration of emotion is disparaged as "touchy-feely." Not everyone will be positive about encouraging emotion in school. Therefore, leaders need to be prepared for difficult dialogue and interesting challenges with faculty and other adults within the school.

More on Communication and Feedback

In Chapter 3, we considered how communication is linked to the idea of personal meaning. If one person believes that he or she has communicated with someone else, yet the other person has not made some sort of personal meaning out of that information, then communication really has not occurred. Lack of communication is one of the biggest stumbling blocks to fostering learning and change in schools.

The issue around communication and feedback is that everyone needs to know, "How are we doing?" That means the first problem to be addressed is, "What are we supposed to be doing?" It seems logical that to know *how* we are doing, we first have to know *what* we are doing. Though this seems simple, it usually turns into an interesting dialogue. People hold diverse opinions about what schools should be doing, what teachers should be doing, what principals should be doing, what students should be doing, and what parents should be doing. Therefore, the first step in communicating about "how we are doing" is to clearly define "what we should be doing." (This clarity is discussed further in Chapter 7.)

Once we agree on what we should be doing, communication and feedback play a significant role in determining how well we are going to do it. Simply put, schools require lots of dialogue. This fact is unavoidable. And when we talk about the important work of schools, we are not talking about a new product, whether or not to go on a vacation, car pooling, getting the roof fixed, taking out the garbage, buying a new car, or getting a new checking account. School communication is about people's lives. We are talking about whether or not kids are learning, teachers are teaching, principals and staff are supporting the teaching and learning, and parents are reinforcing the purpose of the school. This kind of communication is crucial to everyone's learning, and it is the force behind making needed changes in behavior and policies and expectations.

True communication about complex issues of teaching and learning requires us to suspend judgment and talk openly and honestly about the assumptions that drive the work we do and the kinds of evidence we use—or don't use—to know how we are doing. It is a dialogue that must be driven by feedback from everyone involved.

Communication, Feedback, and Student Learning

Teachers, principals, staff members, and parents must ask students about their experience of school. Are they being asked to do enough work, the right kind of work, meaningful work? Do they understand what they are doing and why they are doing it? Are their voices heard in the school? Are their interests advocated? Do they feel empowered with knowledge? Are they challenged rather than threatened, coached rather than ignored? Are they valued and encouraged? Does anyone pay attention to them? Do they participate in conversations about evaluation of their work so they know where their work is strong, where it is lacking, what can be done to improve? Do they see what kinds of direction they must take to get better at what they are doing? Do they see the purpose of their efforts? Are they learning how to monitor and evaluate their own work? Are they learning how to give useful and productive feedback to others? Are all of their needs considered, not just their academics?

This kind of information is crucial in knowing how feedback and communication need to be improved to help students grow. However, we usually rely on tests and grades for feedback to and from students. We don't always value the dialogue that must occur if we are to understand what students truly are learning, perceiving, believing, remembering, and understanding. Nevertheless, we must hear from them how their personal meanings are shifting if we are to offer useful feedback and direction for the future.

To gain this kind of information in schools means that we have to change the way we do things now. There are just so many hours that people can be expected to work, interact, and learn together. It may mean shifting priorities from covering material to making time to hear from students and parents how students are doing. It may mean shifting the task of feedback away from the teacher, making it a task that is shared by students, parents, and teachers alike.

> In one **elementary** program, teachers, students, and parents meet every four weeks to discuss student progress. Parents are expected to attend and be prepared to share informed observations about their children's learning. Teachers are expected to bring documentation of student progress in a variety of areas that have been prioritized in previous conferences. Students are expected to lead these conferences, and they must be prepared to share their own observations about how they are doing. Classes are suspended for a couple of days so that these conferences can take place.
>
> Although formal classes are not conducted during this time, the learning that occurs is obvious. Conversations among students,

teachers, and parents are intense. There is much laughter and celebration of growth, even some tears over continuing frustrations and backsliding. The days are filled with emotion and feeling. Everyone comes away with renewed vigor and purpose along with a sense of direction that is remarkable in students so young and parents and teachers so fatigued. These conferences are a time of renewal, refocused energy, and shared purpose. Everyone believes that these days are some of the best in the school year. Grades are never discussed—teachers simply don't give them!

The **middle school** teachers in this same district do similar evaluations, only not so frequently. They, too, avoid grades in favor of three evaluations: at expected level of performance, above expected level, or below expected level. Again, the idea of a partnership among teacher, student, and parent prevails in these conferences. Students' and parents' inputs are highly valued. Everyone shares ideas about the student's growth and progress in learning, and together they plan which areas will be emphasized before the next conference. Learning contracts are formulated based on these conferences. The tension is a little higher during this time because the teachers do not suspend classes completely, and they hold conferences at night while they still plan for classes during the day. Unlike their elementary colleagues, they believe that they need to keep classes going even though the work they are doing with communication and feedback clearly is important and meaningful to all.

In this same district, the **high school** takes a different approach to communication and feedback. The culture of the high school is built around what kids will need for college, and everyone believes that students need grades to get into college. Though that fact is not really true, there is a prevailing belief system that it is true. Most high school teachers expect students to choose to get a grade in a course, even though they are optional for each class. Thus, grades prevail.

Parents and students are expected to meet with teachers every 12 weeks following each "grading" period. Although these conferences center on a variety of learning issues, the major focus is always what grades students receive in which classes. Tension during this time is extremely high. All the work of feedback and evaluation is done by teachers. Teachers not only have to compute grades for each of the students, they also have to write a narrative to accompany each grade. This work is enormously time-consuming and is added on to the usual work of classes during the day. Some time from classes is set aside, but not much. The week is fraught with tension, exhaustion, and adversarial relationships. It is a nightmare to live through, and most people are just glad to have it over.

Why is feedback so different in the same school system? Perhaps one reason is that educators at one level perceive communication and feedback as an ongoing dialogue among teachers, parents, and students. They see it as a normal, expected, and important part of the learning process. Teachers at another level see communication and feedback as a burden to be taken on and removed as soon as possible. The burden has nothing to do with the learning process; it is merely the burden of reporting in order to appear accountable. This assessment may seem something of an oversimplification of a complex issue, but we cannot overemphasize the importance of communication and feedback in maximizing personal learning.

Communication, Feedback, and Adult Learning

The same kinds of issues surface when discussing how to create a climate where adults can benefit from communication and feedback. There is no need to repeat a discussion of teacher evaluation here. But we need to think about the type of dialogue that is necessary to assure personal learning in adults who work in the school.

In his innovative work on organizational systems, Senge (1990) describes the difference between discussion and dialogue. Both types of communication are important. In most organizations, however, dialogue never occurs; all communication is discussion.

The tenets of discussion are that everyone involved contributes ideas for solving a problem, and the group eventually arrives at what it considers the best solution. In a discussion, there is the condition of having a problem, the need to make a decision, and a climate where people compete for the "best" solution and attempt to persuade others to support their position. In a dialogue, on the other hand, all assumptions are first made clear. Then they're set aside for the remainder of the dialogue. There is no attempt to persuade anyone to support any position. The conversation that follows challenges the *what* and *why* of assumptions, and it encourages everyone to see multiple perspectives and experiences of the situation being reviewed. It is dialogue, not discussion, that fosters the most personal learning and growth.

When people are forced to suspend assumptions, they are put into strange territory where fundamental belief systems will be challenged by others who are doing the same thing. Thinking through the premises of our assumptions and hearing without judgment other equally valid assumptions—these processes create the best climate for new construction of personal meaning. It is difficult work, but it is satisfying because it requires a deep understanding of others' viewpoints. This depth of understanding can lead to closer alignment in carrying out the shared vision of the organization, which in turn leads to greater synergy and accomplishments than would be possible if individuals worked separately to carry out tasks. In fact, Senge (1990) leads us to believe that empowering individuals without also demanding alignment of purpose and vision leads to greater chaos and wasted effort than if leaders did nothing to empower people in the first place.

Cooperation and Collaboration

It should be obvious that powerful communication and feedback require collaboration among all stakeholders. The culture of schools, however, often fosters isolation and individualism, not cooperation and collaboration. Some schools are changing; but cultures die long, hard deaths. Leaders who are "culture breakers" must endure brutal attacks from those who are threatened by change in cultural rules and expectations.

Even the popular media make the destruction of cultural boundaries difficult. Movies extol the virtues of teachers who work as mavericks outside of or against the system to create change. The system, and the leaders of that system, are portrayed as stodgy and unenlightened, forces to be ignored and circumvented. The maverick who challenges the meanness and stupidity of the other people in the school wins out in the end for the forces of good. Flags fly, horns blare, and the mavericks are honored at emotional testimonials. Once again, the virtues of stoic individuals win out over the forces of evil that are incarnate in the "system" of the school.

Is it any wonder that school leaders face difficulties with collaboration? The reality is that collaboration—not competition—leads to greater learning. Competition is the anathema of scholarship. To learn the most, to grow in knowledge and wisdom, people must feel free to explore, to take risks, to challenge their own ideas and those of others in a threat-free environment, to sometimes wander aimlessly in a world of confusion searching for a meaning that will give focus and direction to the content of the learning. None of this suggests competition with others. If the focus is on winning, scholarship becomes narrow and limited in its scope, bounded by artificial and contrived goals. To "beat" someone else in a game has nothing to do with true learning. To seek with others the multiple realities of truth, however, is what scholarship and learning truly are about. This kind of seeking is best done with others in relationships that are characterized by mutual respect and equality, where the joy comes not from "besting" someone but from discovering together a meaning that is fresh and new and gives insight to many other pieces of each others' lives.

The difference between competition and collaboration is similar to the difference Senge (1990) delineates between discussion and dialogue. In discussion, people compete for acceptance of their positions and attempt to persuade others to follow what they suggest. In dialogue, there is no attempt to compete with each other. It is instead a venture into conversation where no assumptions are made, where people explore possibilities and meanings together on an equal footing, and where new insights not imagined before emerge. School is not a game. It is an adventure of discovery. To put learning into the realm of competition is to pit one against another rather than to share enlightenment along the journey.

∽ ∽ ∽

Clearly, establishing a school where true learning and change can occur is difficult work for leaders. Yet educational leaders can serve as models for all the adults who also help to lead schools toward a vision of places of learning. For schools to become places where people come to grow, learn, change, expand, and find joy in discovery, everyone must be seen as a learner with needs to be met. The school community needs to organize around a central theme of meeting people's needs.

To meet people's needs, learning must be challenging, not threatening, and it must be accompanied by strong emotion and feeling so that learners can personalize their learning into new forms of understanding. Communication must be widespread; and it must be open, honest, caring, and helpful about what steps to take next. Most of all, learning must become a collaborative search for multiple realities of truth and understanding.

In a school where concern for learning and change dominates the vision and the daily reality of school life, people see learning as a journey taken together in a climate that supports risk taking. This kind of school does not see learning as an arrival point predetermined by others, for others. Instead, the school arranges itself so that learning needs are met; people feel free from threat; passion for the learning of all people is encouraged; honest communication through supportive dialogue links people in common, aligned goals; and all people feel included through the expectation of cooperative and collaborative work.

THE LEADER'S
SENSE OF SELF

IN CHAPTER 1, WE EMPHASIZED THAT BELIEFS ABOUT SELF
are the most important factors in determining human behavior. How
leaders view themselves influences how they behave and how they
communicate with other people. Views of self also influence how
leaders perceive the teaching and learning process, and they determine how leaders interact with students, teachers, and parents.
In short, the leader's self-concept affects everything that happens in
a school, and it significantly influences relationships with others
in the school community.

A positive view of self is characteristic of a healthy, fully functioning individual. Leaders who hold positive views of self are more
likely to have positive views of other people in the learning environment. They also will be less controlling and develop trust in the
school community. Person-centered psychologists have identified
three major characteristics of a healthy self: having a positive view of
self, maintaining an openness to experience, and possessing a feeling
of oneness and identification with others (Combs, 1962b). These

characteristics allow school leaders to develop and lead a healthy school.

Positive Self-Concept

Self-concept is a person's unique organization of beliefs about who or what he or she is. All of us have many beliefs about ourselves, which we learn through our life experiences. Leaders, too, have acquired beliefs about themselves throughout life, and these beliefs are central to their existence. For example, a school leader may view herself as having expertise in scheduling and budgeting, but she may not feel so positively about her interpersonal relationships with teachers and parents.

Leaders' self-perceptions also have values attached to them. Our self-concept includes not only self-definitions but also the value we place on those definitions. For example, principal Susan Gardner views herself as an excellent disciplinarian. She also believes this role is very important in school life. On the other hand, Susan knows she has poor delegating skills, but she does not place high value on them. Thus, having few delegation skills does not necessarily bother her or diminish her self-concept.

Self-concepts are learned from prior experience and through the interactions we have every day with important people in our lives. Children develop self-concepts largely through interactions with parents or other family members. Children's self-concepts also are developed in school through interactions with teachers, principals, and other students. Experiences with demeaning teachers are likely to affect students' self-concepts negatively. Likewise, students who demean, ridicule, or humiliate other children are likely to influence their own and others' self-concepts negatively.

Leaders' self-concepts also are influenced by prior experiences. Leaders enter their positions with well-developed self-concepts already in place. Chances are that school leaders have fairly positive self-concepts because they have had successful experiences leading up to their selection for their role. More than likely, most school leaders also had fairly successful experiences throughout their education in elementary and secondary school, higher education, and undergraduate and graduate programs.

School leaders' self-concepts are affected by daily experiences, too. The ways in which supervisors, teachers, students, and parents view the leader and the job he or she is doing influence a leader's self-concept. As mentioned in Chapter 1, leaders who see themselves as acceptable and capable behave as though they are. They expect to succeed. Conversely, leaders who believe they are inadequate are more likely to behave tentatively or fearfully, and they will avoid situations that might prove embarrassing.

Benefits of a Positive Self-Concept

A positive view of self offers many advantages for school leaders, schools, and the education profession in general. Leaders who have positive self-concepts feel a greater degree of respect for their own uniqueness. They worry less about conformity and allow themselves to take risks and try innovative approaches because they feel adequate about themselves. In essence, the self does not interfere with events internal and external to the school. For example, when trying new approaches in curriculum, instruction, or scheduling, leaders who feel adequate are more likely to forge ahead with change instead of worrying about how much criticism they will receive from others.

Leaders who feel positive self-regard are less likely to experience stress on the job. They are less disturbed by the criticism associated with their role, and they remain stable because they trust themselves and the actions they take. Moreover, school leaders who see themselves positively are more apt to view problems objectively because they are not constantly worried about protecting their self-concepts. Solutions to problems are perceived as sound and reasonable because the solutions need not be tied to the enhancement of self. Perhaps most importantly, when the self is fulfilled, leaders are better able to respond to others unselfishly and are able to offer enhanced support and empathy for students and staff. These leaders are generous. They give of themselves and become more personally involved in the events of the school and in others' lives.

Conditions Affecting Self-Concept

Though many leaders have positive views of self, it is easy to see how conditions in schools today can modify leaders' self-concepts. Changing social conditions, greater demands for accountability, declining student performance, and declining revenues create significant and challenging issues for administrators.

For example, let's go back to the principal's day again (as begun in Chapter 2). A principal's many responsibilities often create conflict between personal and professional identities.

Faced with demanding pressures, principals and other administrators often don't know where to turn. Even the most secure principal can, at times, feel isolated and lonely. As one high school principal stated, "In this district, administrators are supposed to be in charge. If something goes wrong, I'm responsible. My job is on the line if I can't solve the problem. Being on the line all the time causes a feeling of powerlessness because I can't possibly solve all the variables" (Whitaker, 1996).

Principals are people too. They have spiritual, emotional, and psychological needs, and, despite a reputation of being "thick skinned," principals' self-concepts can be damaged. This is an important point for supervisors of principals—and other administrators—to consider. Often, central office personnel have extremely high—even impossible—expectations of principals. Many principals work 60- and 70-hour weeks trying to balance all the elements that make up a school community. Many principals have pointed out that school leaders can't possibly control all the variables—nor should they be expected to. One negative comment from a supervisor can have a devastating effect on a school leader, as the following example shows.

"Susan, I thought I asked you to make sure your teachers attend the staff development sessions sponsored by the district," said the superintendent. "Do you think you're tough enough to handle this?"

Susan replied, "I thought all the teachers in my building were present at the session. I'll try next time to make sure they are all there."

Susan was devastated that the superintendent implied that she might not be "tough enough" to make sure teachers showed up at the inservice session or that she might not be strong enough to do her job. Although Susan thought she worked collaboratively with teachers, she began to second-guess herself and the manner in which she worked with her teachers. Susan wondered whether she should be much more directive with teachers.

Negative experiences such as the one just described force individuals to be self-concealing rather than self-revealing. Principals' jobs are difficult enough without adding coercive or threatening behaviors from supervisors. When people become self-concealing, they are afraid to share themselves because they fear being wrong or ridiculed for a particular thought or action. Such threatening practices frequently cause people to build walls around themselves, blocking out events and other people. This kind of behavior hinders the development of a positive self and is particularly disturbing as applied to school leaders.

Not only do principals sometimes face insurmountable expectations from supervisors, they face conflicting and often unrealistic expectations from state education agencies, other administrators, teachers, and students. State education agencies and legislatures, for example, mandate policies related to teacher certification, teacher evaluation systems, discipline, and academic standards. Principals' plates are full simply trying to manage all these varying interests without adding micromanaging from the state.

One principal in a district where the school board won a "back to basics" majority faces conflicting pressures from the board, central administration, and parents. Parents were excited about the progressive changes the principal and her staff made in curriculum and assessment. Now the board and the superintendent have instructed her to change direction, to return to the old way of doing things even though she has support from the community. Couple this situation with the fact that the state has mandated adoption of content standards for each district to meet or exceed state standards. What is the principal to do? These kinds of circumstances leave principals second-guessing themselves about which direction to take. This encourages self-concealing behavior and sometimes erodes self-concept.

It can be difficult for principals to maintain a positive view of self with the pressures, conflicts, and demands placed on them. When a principal resolves one conflict, another arises because the resolution angered another constituency. The principal needs a strong self-concept to weather these constant storms. The following scenario illustrates another aspect of the effects of self-concept. Notice how differently each principal behaves.

> A school in a suburb of a major city faces changing demographics. There has been a major influx of low-income families, single-parent families, and minority children. The central administration has noticed a decline in overall student performance in the school. The school climate is rapidly deteriorating, too. Teachers' morale is low because they feel powerless to resolve several complex issues. Parent apathy is readily apparent. The superintendent approaches the new principal to see if he has ideas about how to approach the problem.
>
> The first principal, Jim Snyder, feels **inadequate and unsure** of himself in dealing with the problems. Because of his self-perceptions, he reacts tentatively. Jim feels threatened by the changing demographics and by the superintendent's questions and the pressure to do something to improve the situation. Moreover, he does not perceive that he has the knowledge and skills to improve student performance. These feelings cause Jim to put up defense mechanisms and to have

tunnel vision, preventing him from opening up and viewing the problem more openly. He blames the low performance on the "type of kid" in the school. He avoids student performance and climate issues with teachers, students, and parents. Student performance and school climate continue to plummet.

The second principal is Jan Smedley. She feels **positive** about herself, and she reacts to the situation differently. She does not perceive that the superintendent's questions are threatening at all. Jan also feels that she has the knowledge and skills to develop a plan for improving student performance. Jan does not feel threatened by the complex issues, and she views the situation as a challenge. She brings the dilemma to the attention of staff and community members, and she initiates a series of forums to discuss the implications. She invites ideas for helping students improve performance. Early in the process, Jan points out to staff and community members what a great opportunity they have to demonstrate that *all* students can learn, grow, and excel.

Why did the behaviors of these two principals differ? The answer lies in their self-concepts. The first principal feels inadequate and acts tentatively. He tries to avoid the situation, and he blames other factors for lack of success. Jim's behavior is a result of his feelings of inadequacy and his fear of being perceived as not knowing how to resolve the issue. By contrast, the second principal feels positively about herself. She seizes the opportunity to overcome adversity and challenges herself and the school community to tackle the issues head-on. Jan does not worry much about feeling inadequate or making the wrong decision. Jan behaves as though she expects to succeed, and she expects others to succeed as well. The very existence of such attitudes makes success more likely and confirms her positive sense of self.

These examples demonstrate an important point about self-concept. Leaders need to be aware of how they view themselves, especially when they feel inadequate. As long as he feels inadequate, Jim probably will continue to build a wall around himself to defend his self-concept. His behavior represents the use of defense mechanisms to protect the self. Jim may not even be aware that he is defending his self-concept when he blames others for the students' low performance. And unless Jim becomes aware of these feelings of inadequacy, he probably will be unsuccessful as a principal.

Openness to Experience

A second characteristic of a healthy self is openness to experience, which is a willingness to confront what is present. It is accepting into awareness any and all aspects of reality, not denying reality. Yet a willingness to confront the facts does not mean that a person is overcome by or resigned to them.

An individual's ability to be open to experience is directly related to a positive view of self and freedom from threat. A positive view of self means individuals feel less of a need to erect defense mechanisms; thus, acceptance of reality is easier. When people feel threatened, their perceptions become narrowed. They focus on the threatening events, and they respond with defensive behaviors. We referred to this principle in Chapter 3 as tunnel vision. Perceived threat narrows a person's viewpoint, causing him or her to overlook significant events. Conversely, staying open to all experiences allows individuals to seek more data that might be useful in making better decisions (Combs, 1962b).

Simply put, school leaders are more effective if they are open to experience. Remaining open to experience may be very difficult for principals because they face conflict almost daily. Principals must learn how to face dissension without perceiving it as a "personal attack" on their integrity, beliefs, or decision-making capabilities. If principals perceive threats on a regular basis, their perceptions will be narrowed, and it is likely that effective decision making will be jeopardized.

Fear of making mistakes is common among school leaders. Principals realize that, in some cases, making a mistake can have devastating consequences. Depending on the kind of mistake and its effects on people, it might spark the ire of the superintendent or anger teachers or parents. But leaders who are frequently afraid of making mistakes tie themselves into knots and lower their own capacity for effective decision making. Again, under such circumstances, they narrow their perceptual fields.

Let's examine the concept of openness to experience with an example that many principals face in the evaluation process: deciding what to do about a teacher who is not performing well. In this situation, principals face the dilemma of how to handle a teacher who is detrimental to children. When the principal perceives that a teacher is harmful to children, he or she likely is faced with the decision to terminate or not terminate the teacher. It can be gut-wrenching to watch a teacher who is, in the principal's opinion, harmful to children. But what about the teacher? How long should a principal try to effect a positive change in the teacher before taking more serious action?

This situation is delicate. Because of genuine concern for children's welfare, principals often feel a strong need to be "in control," to act promptly, and to follow prescribed procedures for placing a teacher on remediation or, ultimately, for terminating the teacher. Yet a leader who is open to experience examines what is going on now. He or she takes the time to ascertain his or her own feelings and what the teacher is feeling, without concentrating on prescribed evaluation procedures. These leaders think about doing what is right for children *and* the teacher. They are open to all experiences and feelings relative to the issue, and they give themselves access to as much data as possible. This data might include the teacher's past personal and professional experiences and his or her psychological state, including any personal difficulties. These data can give clues as to why the teacher is ineffective. Other data might include the perceptions of children and their parents. Is the teacher just weak on instructional strategies and classroom management, or is the teacher actually diminishing the children's self-concepts?

A principal who is open to experience is more likely to confront the problem, gather an abundance of data, and find comfort in not making a hasty decision. The data this leader uses will be more accurate and less distorted. A principal who is open to experience accepts the situation and simultaneously works to improve the problem over the long run. Such a principal has the self-concept necessary for a higher tolerance of ambiguity and recognizes that the problem will not be solved easily. The principal works with the teacher and his or her colleagues to try to effect change. With this kind of leadership, the teacher is more likely to change because he or she feels the leader is accepting, nonthreatening, and demonstrating a keen sensitivity. If change does not occur over the long run, the principal has more data to make an intelligent decision about termination.

Conversely, a principal who feels threatened by a low-performing teacher is more likely to exhibit "tunnel vision." He or she will make hasty decisions or overlook facts and circumstances surrounding the issue. When our ability to perceive is narrowed to the threatening object or event, we miss other things that might be important to the situation. Thus, a principal who has tunnel vision and is not open to experience will spend less time gathering data. Because of a heavy reliance on evaluation procedures or a need to be prompt in making a decision, such a leader will be less likely to provide ongoing assistance to the low-performing teacher. Being unable to open up to all the data surrounding the issue and having a desire to "get rid of the problem" immediately, the principal will be less likely to show sensitivity to the teacher.

A leader's ability to be open to experience makes for a more supportive and caring learning environment for adults and children alike. Leaders who are open to experience are sensitive to what is going on in the school environment, sensitive to others' feelings, and sensitive to their own feelings. They are more accepting of various routes to a final destination, and they have a wider repertoire of strategies to use with problems. Focusing on experiences and being open to feelings associated with those experiences helps leaders make thoughtful decisions and confront problems openly.

Identification with Others

A third characteristic of a healthy self is a feeling of identification with others, a topic also discussed in Chapter 3. Effective leaders who have an identification with others empathize with all of humanity without reference to gender, ethnicity, social status, or sexual orientation. They have a feeling of oneness with others, a feeling of belonging, and an extension of self that includes others (Combs, 1962b). They have an authentic concern for others' welfare and a genuine desire to facilitate others in their own growth and development.

Because they have a genuine concern for the welfare of others, effective leaders are more attuned to the feelings of other individuals. Others will see this leader as trustworthy because of his or her high level of concern for them. Research shows over and over that one of the characteristics of effective leadership is trustworthiness. Effective leaders have a high degree of trust in others and others have a high level of trust in them.

Most of us have experienced situations in which a leader did not engender a sense of trust within the organization. Consider the observations of two new teachers about the schools in which they are about to teach.

School A

As Sharon Jones entered school on the first day, she noticed different patterns than she was accustomed to in her student-teaching experience. The staff talked of "our" programs. They seemed to know how decisions were made, and they freely discussed how their ideas influenced the final decision. Individuals seemed to trust and support one another, and they welcomed everyone into the school community. Teachers, support staff, parents, and students seemed to feel positive about themselves and felt a vital part of the school.

In the faculty lounge, teachers communicated across grade levels and disciplines, and they discussed innovative ways to work in inter-disciplinary teams. Mrs. Jones was introduced to her mentor, who helped her get to know others in the school. In the afternoon, the principal spoke to the staff about developing a learning community. The principal also discussed her ideas about how to develop a caring school community and emphasized the need for shared and consensual decision making. She posed a question to each staff member individu-ally to get a sense of their feelings and thoughts: "What do you think our children should look like when they leave our school?" The prin-cipal listened intently to each response.

School B

Mary Jackson entered school on the first day and was eager to learn how it was different from the one in which she had just completed her student teaching. She had been given her assignment and room number and immediately went to her classroom to begin getting ready for school. After a couple of hours she wondered why the teachers didn't stop by to introduce themselves. Suddenly, Mary began to feel very unsure of herself, her new job, and her new school.

The principal finally approached her later in the morning and welcomed her. He indicated that other teachers would help her "learn the ropes." Later that day, the principal held a faculty meeting. He went over all the rules and regulations very carefully and appointed five teachers to serve on the faculty advisory committee. The principal pointed out that the committee was advisory only, and he would have veto power over decisions that were not "in the best interest of the school." Feeling somewhat uncomfortable, Mrs. Jackson wondered how this school could be so different from the one in which she completed her practice teaching.

These examples demonstrate how the beliefs and behaviors of principals can have major effects on the level of trust in a school. In School A, the principal attempted to establish a trusting environ-ment by involving others in decisions, listening to individual teach-ers' responses, and helping the new teacher to feel a part of the school. On the other hand, the principal in School B behaved autocratically and did not engender a culture of trust. This principal didn't help make the new teacher feel a part of the group.

Effective leaders who have a feeling of oneness with others demonstrate sensitivity to their feelings and attitudes. They learn, through a great deal of experience and reflection, to be sensitive to the needs of children, parents, and teachers in the learning environment. Feelings of compassion are an integral part of these leaders' daily lives.

Every day, principals face the struggles of human existence in the lives of children and staff. Some children arrive at school after a night of beating or sexual abuse, or after witnessing a gang shooting. Teachers arrive at school with their own anxieties and personal problems, too. These issues take a heavy toll on the emotional states of school leaders, but compassion for these individuals and their problems is paramount in establishing empathy.

Leaders who have a strong identification with others are able to work harmoniously in a leader or follower role. Literature is replete with articles about the importance of shared leadership, facilitating leadership, and establishing collaborative work cultures within schools. School leaders need enhanced skills to work collaboratively with teachers, parents, and community. Within this context, school leaders, at times, assume a follower role to develop leadership in others. As demonstrated in the following example, effective leaders build relations with others and do not feel it necessary to always prove they are in control.

> An elementary principal who believed in and modeled consensual decision making held a staff meeting to make a decision related to multi-age grouping of students. The principal thought he had consensus and thought he had a commitment from all that no one would block the collective decision of the group. After the staff meeting, the principal was relieved that the group finally decided to group 3rd, 4th, and 5th graders together. The next morning, a 5th-grade teacher entered the principal's office to talk.

"You didn't listen to me yesterday in the meeting," said the teacher.

The principal responded, "To what are you referring?"

"I tried to point out the difficulties I perceived in grouping students from three grade levels, and my comments seemed to be overlooked," responded the teacher.

"But why didn't you clearly indicate that you opposed the idea? You know our norm about consensual decision making. If one person disagrees with the direction, we postpone the decision and continue discussion."

The teacher responded, "I just decided not to say anything further because I felt my comments were being overlooked."

After this conversation, the principal sent a letter to staff that very day indicating that a decision had not been made because at least one individual had reservations about it. This principal needed a great deal of courage to do this because other staff members might see the letter as "weak." It also took courage for the teacher to speak to the principal about her feelings because, in a sense, she questioned the principal's integrity. But it was critical for the principal to send the letter so as not to damage the trusting relationships within the school and to continue to work harmoniously with others. Had the principal brushed aside the teacher's reservations and her feelings of being overlooked, the teacher probably would not have felt a sense of belonging within the school. She would be inclined to speak less rather than speak more openly, and she probably would have sabotaged the plan.

How do leaders learn to feel identification with others? Like self-concept, identification with others is learned through experiences with others as we mature and develop. Leaders who have spent time around individuals who are friendly and helpful are more likely to identify with them. On the other hand, if leaders have spent time with people who have hurt or humiliated them, they are more likely to construct a wall around themselves and avoid genuine interactions with people. Given the demanding role of the principal, it is difficult for principals to avoid building walls around themselves because of conflict and demanding expectations. Despite these demands, caring principals make a conscious effort to be aware of—and maintain— their feelings of identification with others.

The Leader's Belief System

Perceptual psychologists have noted the importance of consistent and open belief systems in developing fully functioning individuals. They stress that healthy individuals have consistent beliefs and values, and they practice these values in their everyday living. Openness to experience contributes to a strong belief system because gathering more data allows for the emergence of broader and stronger values and beliefs. Healthy individuals often go to great lengths to live out their beliefs. Mahatma Gandhi risked starvation so that he could make a statement about his beliefs. People like Gandhi are aware of their attitudes, behaviors, and everyday actions, and they constantly monitor how closely their actions match their beliefs. In addition, such individuals seek feedback from others to assist them in their reflections.

Unfortunately, some educational leaders do not have a firm grounding in who they are or what their values and beliefs are. Some school leaders have no guidelines from which to make crucial decisions affecting children. It is easy to see why this lack of grounding occurs. Although school leaders have been exposed to perceptual psychology in their undergraduate and graduate work, they may not have internalized these theoretical frameworks in everyday practice. Perhaps they did not have opportunities to examine practice in light of theoretical frameworks during their undergraduate or graduate study. Or perhaps they do not have sufficient opportunities to reflect on and talk about these issues in their busy lives at school.

Espoused Versus Actual Theories

Some leaders have been socialized to accept behaviorist practices to such a great extent that they probably do not recognize inconsistencies between what they say they believe and what their daily routines show. Argyris and Schon (1975) indicate that what people say they believe (espoused theory) frequently clashes with what they actually do in practice (theory-in-use).

Consider this example of an espoused theory and a theory-in-use. Most principals indicate that they believe all children can learn, and they often state this as one of their firmly held beliefs about children and schooling. Yet, when we examine school practices, we frequently see tracking of students. Children who are perceived as brighter are placed together with the best teachers while students who are perceived as having fewer abilities are placed with the "slow learners" and the least effective teachers. Further, we observe that these students do not have equal access to certain resources, such as computers. If a principal really believed all children could learn, he or she would not endorse tracking and homogeneous grouping as an everyday practice. He or she would ensure that all children were afforded rich curricular resources, such as equal access to computers.

Person-centered leaders' firm belief systems affect how they interact with others and how they view teaching and learning. Leaders with strong belief systems are more likely to encourage teachers, parents, and students to make choices that are best suited to them as individuals and to respect the choices made by others, even if they disagree with those choices. Leaders with strong belief systems support the development of positive views of self in others and enable teachers and students to accept the uniqueness of self and others. Moreover, these leaders provide rich opportunities for teachers and students to explore their personal beliefs and values, and they encourage the development of behaviors consistent with their beliefs.

Effective leaders constantly reflect on their beliefs and are open and flexible about filtering in new information that might alter their beliefs. Leaders with clearly identified values accept the responsibility that goes with strong convictions. They accept the responsibility of acting in a trustworthy and genuine fashion. They encourage others to become responsible for their own actions as well.

Acting on Beliefs

Effective leaders act on what they believe to be right, including beliefs about what is right in the teaching and learning process. They possess such strong beliefs about what is right that they are not pressured into conformity. School leaders with strong convictions have a sense of security even when things are not going well. Confident that they can withstand others' attacks, they do not feel a need to backtrack from their positions.

Withstanding the attacks of others and maintaining a sense of security is one of the most difficult tasks facing school leaders. In fact, most of us have known administrators who appear to be "all over the place" with their values and beliefs, changing their stance from one week to the next. The conflict and confrontation that often occurs with the public contributes to this situation. For example, many principals face enormous pressures to return to a basic, fundamental approach to schooling that values conformity, teacher-directed learning, standardized tests, and less emphasis on the development of self-concept.

Principals with strong convictions about teaching and learning do not often perceive that they have to conform to the values of others, but they are more accepting of others' values. When principals face the pressures of moving toward a more fundamental approach to teaching and learning, for example, those with firmly held beliefs listen attentively to their critics, but they stay their course in regard to their own values. It may turn out that eventually a principal must leave a particular job to avoid compromising his or her beliefs. Yet if this occurs, the principal with firmly held values remains secure in the knowledge that he or she made the right decision.

Although it is important for leaders to have consistent and firmly held beliefs, effective leaders also find value in mistakes. They do not assume they are always right, and they are flexible enough to admit mistakes and see the way for improvements and different ways of doing things. These leaders learn from their errors and past experiences, and they are open to new ways of thinking as well as different experiences and relationships. This enables their beliefs to continue to develop.

How do leaders develop consistent belief systems? Leaders' values, of course, develop over time. Some leaders are aware of their beliefs and how they relate to everyday practice. Others are not. It takes a conscious effort to become aware of our belief systems, and it is not an easy task. Engaging in reflection, dialogue, and feedback with others helps individuals explore their beliefs. Examining specific actions on a daily basis is another way to become more conscious of values and how they relate to practices.

Educational Platforms

One way leaders express their values and beliefs is through the development of an educational platform. An educational platform is a "series of assumptions or beliefs usually expressed in declarative, or sometimes normative statements. These assumptions or beliefs deal with the way children and youth grow, with the purposes of schooling, with the nature of learning, with pedagogy or teaching, with educational programs, and with school climate" (Sergiovanni & Starratt, 1979, p. 214).

The platform is a useful tool for educators to use to articulate their educational philosophies. It can help create consistency between espoused beliefs and daily actions. The platform is not a statement of beliefs etched in stone, but it is a foundation that helps leaders articulate a set of beliefs and then revisit them as they encounter additional experiences.

Educational platforms can take several formats. The particular format used doesn't matter. Sergiovanni and Starratt (1979), for example, advocate articulating beliefs about the following:

1. The aims of education.
2. The major achievements desired of students.
3. The social significance of student's learning.
4. The image of the learner.
5. The value of a curriculum.
6. The image of the teacher.
7. The preferred kind of pedagogy.
8. The primary language of discourse in learning situations.
9. The preferred kind of student-teacher relationship.
10. The preferred kind of school climate.
11. The purposes of supervision.
12. The preferred process of supervision.

Although the format and content of educational platforms may differ, all platforms offer an avenue for school leaders to articulate what they value and believe about teaching, learning, and leading. Then they can use the platform to determine how closely their espoused beliefs match their daily practices. School leaders might even share their platforms with other staff members and ask for feedback on the extent to which the platform matches their daily actions. Though this exercise can be somewhat intimidating, effective leaders desire feedback, are open to their experiences, and are secure in obtaining that feedback for their personal and professional growth. This activity also might prove useful for an entire staff, as long as it is conducted in a nonthreatening, supportive environment. Further, the exercise might yield valuable results for an entire school community and could be the basis for significant changes in curriculum, instruction, or assessment.

Research points to the benefits of developing an educational platform:

- An improved ability to reflect, gain self-understanding, and monitor personal actions.
- A greater awareness of and openness to new ideas.

- Broad shifts in perspectives, particularly a sensitivity to others' viewpoints.
- Increased self-confidence and professional commitment.
- An enhanced capacity to match personal goals with current and future job requirements.
- An extension of personal learning to others in the workplace so that they can obtain descriptive feedback and examine possible discrepancies between their intentions and actions (Osterman & Kottkamp, 1993).

Developing a platform can help school leaders increase their self-confidence, enhance openness to experience, develop reflectivity about beliefs and actions, and heighten sensitivity to others' viewpoints. These characteristics are important for the development of the leader's self. Perhaps the value of articulating a platform is best described by a teacher who was preparing to be a school principal:

> I stopped thinking and behaving as a teacher. I started to act as a leader. . . . My classroom behavior changed. I stopped thinking "control" and started thinking "leadership." . . . Students now vote on topics we as a class will learn. Students know they are being heard and heeded.

ॐ ॐ ॐ

This chapter has focused on the characteristics of a healthy self as it applies to educational leaders. Having a positive view of self, maintaining and developing an openness to experience, and possessing a feeling of oneness with others are hallmarks of effective leaders.

It is not easy for leaders to develop a healthy self. School leaders bring to the role emotional baggage, personal issues, and feelings of inadequacy just as other individuals in other roles do. Added to the leader's personal experiences is the impact of the complexity of their role. Conflicting expectations from supervisors, board members, parents, and teachers enhance this complexity. A long tradition of focusing on things rather than people also contributes to the difficulties of maintaining a healthy self.

School leaders have such a moral obligation to assist in the growth and development of children and adults that an increased awareness of self is extremely important. The school leader's self-concept influences everything from reactions to supervisors to teacher evaluation to views on student learning and performance. The leader's positive view of self is directly related to the degree to which he or she accepts others. Having a positive view of self enables authentic, trusting, and lasting relationships with others.

It also is important for school leaders to have an openness to experience. Opening ourselves to new experiences, data, and attitudes allows us to make more thoughtful decisions. Principals who are open to experience are better able to withstand the complexities of the job because they accept into their awareness the reality of the job without feeling guilt that they cannot be "all things to all people."

Leaders also must foster a genuine feeling of identification with others. School leaders who possess a feeling of oneness with others are more likely to exhibit responsible and trustworthy behavior. Such leaders recognize that healthy school environments promote collaboration, cooperation, and interdependence. Although feeling a oneness with others may produce some emotional wear and tear on school leaders, they strive to develop a sense of belonging in the school because they realize that satisfying relationships with others enhance individual growth.

Last, we emphasized the importance of the leader's belief system. As demanding and confusing as the leader's role is today, a firm grounding in values and beliefs serves as an anchor. The leader's belief system influences the myriad of daily practices in schools. Grouping arrangements, scheduling, decision frameworks, discipline systems, staff evaluation, curriculum, instruction, assessment, and a host of other issues are all affected by the leader's beliefs and values. The next chapter addresses the leader's role in developing the self of others. Although it is important for leaders to develop a healthy self, it is equally important for leaders to assist in the development of a healthy self in others.

6
DEVELOPING THE SELF
IN OTHERS

IT IS NOT ENOUGH FOR LEADERS TO POSSESS THE CHARACTERISTICS
of a healthy self. An effective leader also helps develop those characteristics in others within the school environment. For leaders to aid
others in their self-development, they must have positive beliefs
about human motivation and human capacities. Effective leaders
believe that people are able and treat them as such.

Positive Beliefs About People

Research on effective and ineffective helpers demonstrates that
effective helpers perceive people as able and worthy; less effective
helpers perceive individuals as unable, unworthy, or lacking. Moreover, such research shows that effective helpers view human beings
as trustworthy and dependable, while less effective helpers view
others as untrustworthy and undependable (Combs, 1986).

People learn that they are adequate and able from being treated
as if they were. But we can cite many examples of how school leaders
have not treated others as able and worthy. For example, asking

teachers to sign in and out of the school building implies that teachers need to be closely supervised or they will not perform well. Providing teachers with prescriptive instructional and assessment methods to make sure everyone teaches the same way to a specific content standard also demonstrates a lack of trust. Specifying classroom rules about student behavior is another example of treating teachers as unable.

Often, such rules are put into place for what seem like good reasons, without regard to how they might be viewed by those who must enforce them. Moreover, these practices do not provide teachers with an awareness of what it means to be a professional. They don't show teachers that they are able and worthy and can make appropriate decisions for their professional lives and for their classrooms.

Many school practices point to assumptions that students are not able or worthy, either. Some believe that students will naturally get into trouble if there aren't tight rules with punishments attached to keep students "in line." Schools continue to tighten the rein on secondary students to make sure they are in class six periods per day and do not leave school. Many rules keep students inside the school building from 8 a.m. to 3 p.m. These kinds of practices lead some students to refer to schools as "prisons." If students do indeed perceive schools to be prisons, they are unlikely to achieve greater awareness of themselves and the world in which they live while they are in them.

According to person-centered psychology, most people will choose what is healthy for their growth if the way seems open for them to do so. Most of us have a desire to grow and become healthy. The key for school leaders is to open the path for students and staff to grow. Expanding people's horizons means allowing them the freedom to seek what they need. School leaders can help create conditions that are conducive to actualizing the positive nature of students and staff through leadership behaviors that are facilitating, assisting, and encouraging. These behaviors help others seek their potential as human beings.

When school leaders treat staff members as though they are important, responsible, and worthy of respect, these staff members are likely to feel more autonomous and professional. School leaders who treat staff members as if they are trustworthy work collaboratively with them on school problems, genuinely solicit their professional opinions on school-related matters, and show an authentic interest in them as people as well as professionals. This is illustrated in the following scenario. The principal, Mrs. Livingston, shows how a trusting leader might act.

> **Mrs. Livingston:** We have a problem to resolve concerning the number of children in our school who are at or below the poverty level. I feel we need to address the issues these children bring with them to school in a different manner from how we are currently handling them.
>
> **Teacher 1:** These children need lots of different kinds of services that we cannot provide in our current structure.
>
> **Teacher 2:** Perhaps we can contact other community agencies who might be willing to brainstorm possible community responses that would help us with our problem.
>
> **Teacher 3:** Yes, and perhaps we can explore the idea of writing a grant to obtain additional funding for additional services.
>
> **Mrs. Livingston:** These are all wonderful ideas. Let's think about what the next steps are.
>
> **Teacher 1:** What about forming a planning committee to continue brainstorming ideas about contacting key community agencies?
>
> **Mrs. Livingston:** Would someone be willing to facilitate the planning committee?

The principal in this short scenario approached the issue openly and solicited ideas from several staff members. She was willing to empower them to lead the planning group, and she modeled a collaborative approach to resolving a problem. It is evident that she trusts staff members to form ideas about tackling the issue.

Leaders who are trusting also have the obligation to nurture a school environment where students are trusted and viewed as able and worthy. In schools where students are assumed to be able, they can explore, make choices, and involve themselves in decision making. Such an environment allows students a high degree of choice in the learning experiences they select. Some students might choose to leave school and participate in a community project. Others might decide to work with a mentor for part of the day, learning business or technology skills. Other students might decide to become involved in the school's governance process by serving on the shared decision-making council. The possibilities are endless.

We frequently hear that it is the responsibility of school leaders to motivate teachers and students. Some principals actually are held accountable for motivating staff and students. Workshops, conferences, and educational literature are replete with information on how best to motivate others in the school. Often, when we ask school administrators what their greatest concern is, many respond that motivating teachers and students is a challenge.

Teachers cannot make students learn, nor can principals make teachers or students learn or be motivated. To believe they *can* make others learn taps into beliefs associated with behaviorist psychology. Using these premises, motivation becomes the process of getting others to do what someone or some group wants them to do. We have seen many examples of how such behaviorist practices have permeated schools. For example, consider how Mr. Davis, a principal, attempts to motivate his staff to attend an inservice session:

> "You all know that this Friday will be a required inservice day at school. The topic will be how to motivate students to learn. We have a motivational speaker who will be with us all morning. You will be required to sign in when you arrive at 8:00."

What kind of message is this principal's behavior sending? He may believe he is sending a message of concern about student motivation, but it is possible that the only messages faculty members will hear are "required" and "sign in." Such assumptions and practices do little to motivate teachers or students to engage in learning or become the best they can be.

According to perceptual psychology, *motivation is an internal matter of individual wants, desires, needs, fears, and aspirations*. People have a fundamental drive toward health, and they will always try to move toward the maintenance and enhancement of self if the way is open for them to do so (Combs, 1962a). Thus, human beings are always motivated, but they may not necessarily be motivated to do the things others want them to do.

The teacher who decides to skip an inservice session is not unmotivated; rather, she is motivated to do something else with her time. She might decide to spend her time visiting another school, working in her classroom, or exercising. Those are the things that motivate her.

School leaders who do not believe that staff and students are able and can accept responsibility cannot develop trusting environments. This notion has many implications for shared decision making. For many years we assumed that most decisions in a school should be made by administrators. Although this practice is changing, some teachers still are left out of meaningful decisions about substantive work of the school, such as curriculum, instructional methods, assessment, student grouping, and the uses of time during the day. Teachers still face the obstacles of having to follow directives from state departments of education, central office administrators, school board members, or principals.

One middle school principal was quoted as saying,

> We [administrators] have lost all our authority with shared decision making. We are supposed to answer to everyone else and please everyone else and aren't supposed to say "no."

Contrast this comment with one made by a high school principal who valued shared decisions:

> We have 150 talented staff members in this school. It would be senseless to think that I know it all.

Listening to the voices of students and parents is part of establishing a trusting environment. School leaders who model democratic principles show evidence of genuinely accepting students as they are. We can point to many examples of ways principals demonstrate that students are worthy of respect. Here's one example:

> A new principal listened to student objections to a metal detector and got rid of it. Although this principal was concerned about student safety, she realized she needed to demonstrate that student voices were being heard. In so doing, she invited lengthy classroom discussions about how to keep weapons away from school, and she arranged group discussions with students and parents. She also invited community members to offer suggestions for how to tackle the issue. Students ultimately decided they wanted a suggestion box where they could anonymously report anyone suspected of carrying a weapon.

By her actions, this principal sent the message that students, teachers, parents, and community members were valued and that their views mattered. Together, they chose a way to address a problem.

Human Motivation and Self-Concept

We cannot overemphasize that the beliefs school leaders hold about human beings are important in the teaching and learning process. School leaders help create the conditions that will assist teachers and students in their drive toward health and fulfillment. Just as physicians remove diseased organs to improve the physical well being of individuals, school leaders can help remove the barriers to people's needs for fulfillment. Effective school leaders find ways to eliminate some of the controls placed on teachers so that they can work with students to achieve an enhanced awareness of themselves and the world around them.

Developing the Self-Concepts of Others

The need to maintain and enhance the self toward growth and fulfillment is so important that individuals go to great lengths to maintain their self-concepts. In Chapter 5 we noted how the leader's self-concept affects everything that happens in a school. Not only should leaders be keenly aware of developing and maintaining their own self-concepts, but they should also be aware of how important the self-concept is to others and help individuals seek the way toward health and fulfillment. The self-concept is precious to everyone, and we see this manifested in individual behaviors every minute of every day.

Self-concepts are fragile. School leaders often are faced with problematic behaviors of teachers and students that are a result of their feelings about themselves. For example:

> One principal received an evening call from a teacher who was contemplating suicide. The principal vaguely knew this teacher was experiencing some personal problems, but he had no idea the teacher perceived the problems to be so severe that she would contemplate suicide. As the principal became more aware of the teacher's problems, he found out the teacher simply had no confidence that she could continue to face life. She desperately wanted to avoid the misery and conflict she felt within.

This example shows how a lack of awareness about others has the potential to lead to devastating results. As the principal in this scenario later stated, "I had no idea when I became principal that I would hear teachers break into tears in my office over very personal and emotional issues. They don't tell you about these things in principal preparation programs."

Enhancing Student Self-Concept

People behave according to how they see themselves and how they view the world around them. Effective teachers and principals, therefore, concentrate on building and maintaining students' self-concepts. Many studies point to the fact that students who see themselves in positive ways learn better and achieve more (Purkey, 1970). However, the importance of developing student self-concept remains a controversial issue.

Critics cite several reasons that self-concept should not be emphasized in schools. Some believe that a focus on self-concept takes away from academics. Others think that encouraging students to accept themselves leads to self-satisfaction, thus discouraging students from putting forth their best efforts. Still other critics believe that self-concept is a natural outgrowth of achievement so that educators should stress academic performance exclusively (Kohn, 1994). In other words, many critics believe that the self-concept will develop naturally because students feel positive about their academics. Many studies point to the fact that students who see themselves in positive ways learn better and achieve more.

Common sense tells us that society is much better off with individuals who have positive rather than poor self-concepts. People with positive self-concepts base their decisions on more global needs rather than personal ones. They view others in more positive ways and treat them with more respect and dignity. Moreover, a positive self-concept leads people to approach problems with optimism and high ideals. They give more freely to others to help them become healthier and happier.

Self-concept plays a major role in how students view the learning process, too. For example, assessment data frequently demonstrate that girls do not perform as well as boys in math. This often is the result of a girl's belief that she "can't do math." Thus, the girl avoids math, which leads to even poorer performance until finally the student gives up on math. The "self-fulfilling prophecy" takes hold, and the student continues to believe she is poor in math. She may avoid math for many years to come. School leaders can have an enormous influence on altering students' negative self-perceptions, but doing so requires much individualized attention.

Several school practices actually diminish students' self-concepts. A common assumption is that failure is good for everyone, and failure actually enhances motivation. Research in the area of perceptual psychology demonstrates that healthy people see themselves in positive ways. The reason healthy people see themselves in positive ways is that they have experienced success—not failure. Success strengthens individuals, and failure weakens them. The effect of this idea is aptly stated by Astuto and colleagues (1994): "Systems that identify losers, with clear evidence of the extent of their failure, violate principles of effective teaching and learning" (p. 45).

The U.S. educational system spends a good deal of time identifying losers rather than pointing to the successes and gains. This kind of system creates individuals who focus on limitations rather than possibilities, who hesitate to take risks or to innovate and create, and who put others down to feel more elevated themselves.

Grades. Grading is a practice that labels losers and diminishes students' self-concepts. For decades, we have used grading systems as external inducements to get students to do their work. An underlying assumption is that schoolwork is boring. Unless there are external means for making students complete their work, the work will not get done. In other words, people must be made to do things. A failing grade is an example of a threat to get students to work harder. Failing grades may motivate a few students to work harder—but not all of them. And even if a failing grade causes students to work harder for a short period of time, the effect on the self-concept still can be quite negative.

Grades motivate some students some of the time. But many students do not want to be judged or do not want to fail. Thus, they do not get involved in academics. For example:

> A seemingly bored male student was sitting in an Algebra I class one afternoon. A visitor asked the teacher about the boy and why he was sitting by the window alone. The teacher responded, "I just leave him there because he is hopelessly behind in his work and cannot

possibly catch up." The teacher further indicated that the student would definitely receive an F at the end of the semester, which was more than two months away!

Forcing the boy to sit in class for so much time just to receive an F didn't make any sense to the visitor. She pleaded with the teacher to think of something else the student could do during Algebra I class, to treat the boy as a person and make some kind of human response to him. Eventually, the visitor helped the student find something more productive to do with his time.

This case is just one example of how grades are misused and how they actually can diminish self-concept. This math student's failure was much bigger than Algebra I, and the waste of time for him enormous, considering all the meaningful work he could have done. This student probably felt anger, resentment, and alienation, the very characteristics most educators try to avoid creating in schools.

The teacher was obviously not motivated to help the student. Her own self-concept was probably lacking. She therefore treated this student as if he were an object, rather than a human being with needs and desires.

It is the school leader's responsibility to create an awareness about what grades mean, how students are motivated, and how teachers can create work that has greater meaning. To enhance growth and fulfillment, it is necessary for teachers and administrators to provide students with opportunities to spend as much or as little time as necessary in attaining skills and concepts. This individualized approach allows learners to challenge themselves rather than compare their accomplishments to others.

Children have unique personalities with varying needs, interests, and abilities. The wonderful thing about human beings is that they are unique. Teachers and principals alike must create learning environments that foster creative and independent thinking, develop children's awareness of personal growth, and provide opportunities to master basic skills. Teachers also have the responsibility to assess student work and provide feedback so that improvements are made without arbitrary grading systems.

Chapter 3 elaborated on the importance of feedback and highlighted several criteria that make feedback meaningful.

- Feedback should be immediate.
- Feedback should be personal, not comparative.
- Feedback should be directly related to the event.
- Feedback should point the way to next steps.

Grades do not meet any of these criteria. They usually are not immediate or related directly to a specific event. They are comparative rather than personal. They do not point the way to next steps. To better nurture students' self-concepts, leaders can implement strategies of feedback to parents and students through more qualitative and descriptive measures. Portfolios, parent-teacher conferences, and narrative accounts of student work are qualitative measures that provide useful feedback to students and parents alike.

Discipline Methods. The discipline methods prevalent in many schools also diminish, rather than enhance or maintain, student self-concepts. Many discipline systems are punitive, and schools that develop punitive discipline strategies view discipline as a mechanism to control behavior. They don't see it as a process to enhance student growth toward fulfillment of needs. Educators use corporal punishment, detention, in-school and out-of-school suspension, and a host of other practices to deter unwanted student behavior.

Although suspensions certainly are necessary in some instances because of safety issues, such practices often diminish student self-concept, thereby ensuring the repetition of inappropriate behavior. Punishing practices also fail to provide learning experiences, and they rarely deter negative behaviors. Punitive methods also keep students dependent on external controls for too long so that the real lessons of life aren't learned. Again, we are falling back to behaviorist philosophy when we try to condition students to behave in desir-able ways and to conform to the norms and rules of the school. Rigid control of student behavior often leads to feelings of resent-ment and anxiety, especially among high school students, who are developmentally attempting to establish independence. This idea is demonstrated in the following example of how two different principals handled an incident between two students who were openly too affectionate.

Scenario One

Mark Jenkins, the principal, walks up to two students and grabs the young man by the collar. He yells loudly that the students are breaking school policy. The principal demands that the two students report to the office and face suspension. The students tell the principal they are married, but later they are still suspended.

Scenario Two

Brenda White, the principal, walks up to two students. Quietly, in their native Spanish, she speaks to the couple about why some of their behavior is inappropriate. All are smiling by the end of the conversation. The students confide in the principal that they are married, and she congratulates the young couple. The principal later tells an observer, "Sometimes these kids do things I don't think are smart, and sometimes they violate my personal values. But you just have to accept them. You can't be judgmental in this job."

It is easy to see the differences in how these two principals responded to the students' inappropriate behavior. The first principal was judgmental, controlling, and condemning. This approach would not preserve the self-concepts of these students, nor would it enhance his own self-concept as he behaved judgmentally and autocratically. Often people with poor self-concepts feel a strong need to control other people. Developing the self-concept would likely yield behavior that is much less controlling of others.

In the second scenario, the principal was accepting and preserved the dignity and self-concepts of the young people. Yet she still made her point about the inappropriate behavior.

Life's lessons are learned by living, making decisions, making mistakes, and processing experience. Effective discipline systems enable students to learn the lessons of life while preserving their self-concepts. School environments that facilitate student growth provide experiences that lead to self-direction, self-discipline, and self-motivation. Having a voice in setting classroom and school rules and goals empowers students to share in the control of the school environment and to contribute to their self-development.

Teachers, administrators, and students' share the responsibility for maintaining a cooperative and safe environment for everyone. Students generally will strive to create a cooperative atmosphere if they're given the chance to do so. However, often we are too afraid to allow students the opportunity to create a positive environment. We bow to our fears and miss the chance to provide relevant and interesting experiences for students to examine their own beliefs and behaviors—and their impact on the school community.

Enhancing Teacher Self-Concept

Many times, principals overlook the importance of developing teacher self-concept. Excellent teachers see themselves in positive ways. They see themselves as able, liked, and wanted, as people with dignity and integrity. Caring, sensitive, and empathic school leaders contribute to these positive feelings teachers have about themselves.

The degree to which teachers accept themselves affects how they accept students. In many cases, teachers unknowingly punish students because the students have hurt the teachers' self-concepts. For example:

> While watching students complete their work, Mrs. Jackson walks
> up to Johnny. Johnny throws his paper at Mrs. Jackson and yells, "This
> work is so stupid! Why do you give us such stupid busywork to do?"

> Mrs. Jackson immediately sends Johnny to the office for being disruptive in class and not completing his work. As a result, Johnny feels bad about not doing his work and getting sent to the office, and the teacher's self-concept is negatively affected by what Johnny said about the work she provided to the class.

Sometimes school administrators diminish teachers' self-concepts. They demonstrate that they do not trust teachers by controlling and manipulating them. In addition, local and state monitoring and accountability systems, teacher competency testing, and heavy-handed supervision and evaluation all assume that teachers need to have their professional lives externally controlled. In reality, teachers need autonomy to make professional decisions affecting their work with students. Imposing controls and reducing professional autonomy diminishes teachers' feelings of dignity and integrity. This, in turn, diminishes teachers' self-concept.

Evaluation That Diminishes Self-Concept

Teacher evaluation schemes are a prime example of an external control that limits freedom and autonomy. These evaluation models are based on assumptions that teachers must be told how to behave and what instructional techniques and tools to use. Though they are designed to improve teaching and, ultimately, student performance, many evaluation models also are based on an assumption that teaching is a technical skill. They don't see teaching as a set of broad-based skills, knowledge, and understandings that characterize the teacher's professional expertise.

Technical skills include such things as implementation of specific instructional methods and delivery of content from a well-packaged curriculum guide. But if we assume that teachers have professional expertise, we also assume they possess a repertoire of instructional options, know how to create meaningful and relevant learning experiences for students, are sensitive to student needs, and understand child development and learning theories. If teachers do indeed have professional expertise, there is little need to "package" curriculum and instruction for teachers to follow. There also is little need to engage in strict supervision to make sure teachers are following prescribed strategies.

Underlying most teacher evaluation systems is the presumption that quality performance requires administrative supervision. This belief produces models that are highly bureaucratic and control-oriented. Such models also assume that teachers do not have the professional expertise to do their jobs, that individuals are only externally motivated, and that they need the "carrot and the stick" approach to do a good job. These practices diminish teacher self-concept and contribute to the view that teaching is an occupation, not a profession.

Consider the control-oriented evaluation system in place in a large southern state:

> In this state, teachers are evaluated on very specific technical skills, such as stating objectives of the lesson and reaching closure. The evaluation form is in numerical format. Points are given for meeting as many as 50 specific behaviors listed on the observation form. On the final evaluation form, teachers are rated according to a numerical scale where 1 is *deficient* and 5 is *outstanding*. Teachers who "score" a 4.5 or higher are provided with career ladder funds to supplement their base salary.

This numeric system produces robotic behavior in teachers and does little to contribute to professional growth. Robotic behavior also produces a void, unquestioned acceptance of authority, a dependence on external forces, and a loss of creativity. This kind of evaluation process is an excellent example of the manipulation-of-forces approach to education discussed in Chapter 1.

Person-Centered Evaluation

If controlling evaluation systems don't produce growth, what kind of model makes sense? The person-centered approach advocates evaluation models where collaboration among colleagues enriches professional decision making. Teachers and school leaders have opportunities to collaborate about the crucial decisions that affect student learning, and they have meaningful dialogue about important issues. This kind of atmosphere focuses on the human side of learning rather than the technical side.

Sometimes we make the mistake of viewing teaching as only what occurs in the classroom. Being a professional teacher encompasses reflection, professional growth, mentoring other teachers, and developing curriculum and assessment to assist the profession as a whole. In a collaborative learning community, teachers freely observe one another and provide meaningful feedback. Teachers and administrators work together to develop teaching materials and activities. They support one another in trying creative and innovative approaches, and they engage in frequent dialogue about what is happening in the learning environment. In collaborative environments, teachers work in teams to make decisions affecting their own and their students' work. Unless teachers, students, parents, and school leaders really talk to one another on a regular basis, growth is diminished.

Teachers and principals *do* need feedback to contribute to their professional growth. In fact, processes like peer evaluation or peer coaching contribute a great deal to the growth of teachers and administrators. Peer evaluation is a process where teachers, rather than administrators, take formal responsibility for assessing their peers' progress and providing constructive feedback. With peer coaching, feedback is for formative growth only, not formal evaluation.

These processes offer feedback and support in a nonthreatening environment. They actually can enhance teacher self-concept. Peer assessment models also help teachers feel less isolated, and they increase collegial interactions among teachers and administrators. When fear is removed from the evaluation system, teachers begin to view themselves as good teachers, and enhanced growth emerges. A teacher who is having difficulties in the classroom needs helpful feedback and guidance from supportive peers, not an administrator giving a low score on an evaluation instrument.

Enlightened school leaders value professional and personal growth, and they remove barriers to that growth. These leaders know teachers well enough to understand their true needs. This requires a tremendous amount of dialogue and sharing. Authentic dialogue and sharing with one another are prerequisites to cultivating an openness to experience.

Developing Openness to Experience

In Chapter 4 we described why it is important for leaders to be open to experience. Adept leaders assist others in developing an openness to experience, too. Individuals who are open to experience are sensitive to what is going on in the environment, sensitive to what is going on with others, and sensitive to their own feelings and reactions (Rogers, 1962). Leaders who have an openness to experience develop fewer defense mechanisms and are more open to a variety of data to assist in personal growth. Perhaps most important, individuals who develop openness to experience value creativity.

Students and Openness to Experience

The degree to which people have creativity is directly related to the degree of freedom they are provided. Developing an openness to experience naturally means removing barriers that inhibit creativity. Examples of these barriers include a focus on authority, a preoccupation with the "right way," lack of trust, and an emphasis on controlling others through threats and coercion. Principals and teachers have a joint responsibility to remove these barriers. If creativity is desired, we cannot also expect conformity. When conformity is desired, creativity is hampered. The following description of a large high school illustrates how some schools severely limit creativity and openness.

A large suburban high school enrolls 2,600 students. The high school has four grades, 9–12, and a traditional schedule. Each student has six 55-minute classes. Most courses are required so that students can obtain the 24 credits needed for graduation. Students get schedules at registration time. Teacher names are provided for the required courses. Students also are provided a copy of the State Discipline Management Plan, which details specific consequences for misbehavior.

Most classes have 30 students, and teachers routinely engage in lecture and seatwork. The campus is "closed," which means that students cannot leave school even during lunchtime. There is a parking attendant at the gate who allows students to leave at designated times. The school has many policies regarding attendance, tardies, grades, student activities, and dress.

This is only a brief description of a few practices in one high school. But this description easily could describe many high schools today. In this kind of environment, creativity is hampered rather than encouraged, and conformity prevails. Students, administrators, and staff are obsessed with rules, regulations, and policies. They spend an inordinate amount of time making sure everyone conforms to these policies. Threat and coercion are emphasized by the discipline management plan and the closed campus. Students and staff find little freedom in this school. Creativity and openness are limited.

One of the ways school leaders can promote creativity is by encouraging flexibility, which encourages creative behavior. For example, students might be offered flexible arrangements in curricular offerings, in scheduling and grouping, in teacher-student interactions, in physical structures, and in the development of school goals and policies. Yet in recent years, with the advent of more stringent graduation requirements, electives have been reduced. Many students have few opportunities to explore content that really excites them.

Although many elementary and middle schools have moved away from homogeneous grouping of students to multi-age grouping, many secondary schools have maintained traditional grouping and scheduling of students, which reinforces tracking and limits students' flexibility. Many schools still have several 45- or 55-minute class periods of required coursework where students are identified with a single grade level. Instead, multidisciplinary, cross-age groupings, in which students are given larger blocks of time to explore issues in depth, enhance motivation and creativity.

School leaders have a responsibility to foster student risk-taking so that children have experiences that challenge them to problem solve, think critically, evaluate data, and support their decisions. If students are encouraged to think critically, they will question school policies more often. They'll also be more active in finding solutions to school issues. Students in environments that encourage risk taking are inspired to debate critical issues with classmates, principals, and teachers in a nonthreatening, respectful manner. For example, students in one high school challenged an oil company about waste the company dumped in a river. The students ended up in a year-long science project involving a clean-up of the river. They also were involved in legal issues to correct the problem. What a learning experience!

Staff and Openness to Experience

School leaders who foster creativity also provide choices for teachers and other staff members. Rather than hold teachers to stringent rules regarding grading, instructional practices, or evaluation models, leaders model risk-taking by allowing teachers to generate different and more flexible systems. For example, teachers might be encouraged to develop alternative assessment practices. Or teachers might be encouraged to organize into teaching teams, working with different groups of students on differentiated work. Principals can encourage the development of peer feedback arrangements. All these examples point to the leader's role in fostering creativity and openness in staff members. Leaders who model risk-taking and flexibility establish them as norms in the school—not exceptions.

Developing openness to experience depends on risk-taking and innovation. Many professional educators want to find creative innovations that address school issues, provided there are no negative consequences. Teachers do not demand total safety, only assurance that their creative efforts will not single them out for negative repercussions. For some teachers, just knowing the principal will not vacillate in providing support for new ideas and practices is enough to keep them going. Others might require more frequent assurance. By establishing a norm of risk-taking and creativity, effective leaders provide emotional support for the initiators of creative practices and pave the way for others to follow.

In addition to fostering risk-taking and creativity, effective leaders model facilitating behaviors. These leaders serve as guides, helpers, and supporters of learning and growth. These leaders are not control-oriented or manipulative with others, but they develop a collaborative and professional school culture where others participate in the important decisions affecting the school. When these behaviors are in place, we begin to see more enthusiasm, commitment, and creativity, as well as a sense of community within a school.

Most people want to be involved. By genuinely involving others in the important issues facing the school, facilitative leaders model open communication where problem solving occurs. They help staff members and the community focus on broader issues facing the school. For example, teachers pay close attention to the kinds of agenda items discussed in faculty meetings, and agenda items often show what is really valued in the school. Principals who focus on narrow and mundane items frequently spend time in meetings reinforcing various school policies. They don't spend time in dialogue about enhancing student and staff growth. Unfortunately, many educators would experience culture shock if they participated in a faculty meeting with dialogue about helping people grow!

School leaders have the obligation to invite others to participate in the leadership of the school. They can help teachers develop their leadership skills and work to create new leadership structures, a term Sergiovanni (1994) refers to as "leadership density." As one teacher who worked with a facilitative principal stated:

> My principal really included the school community in the development of our school vision. The effect of this inclusiveness seemed to be a greater openness among the faculty to each other's ideas and a decreased defensiveness toward the accomplishments of colleagues.

It takes a good deal of time and a change in school culture for genuine openness to occur among staff members. Skillful leaders consciously direct their attention to this idea so that the school culture gradually changes over time.

Teachers have a role in facilitative leadership, too. As principals model facilitative behaviors, teachers are more likely to become more facilitative in the classroom. For decades, the role of teachers has been dispenser of information. The curriculum has been viewed as something to be "covered" rather than "discovered." By incorporating some of the ideas we have suggested, perhaps school cultures can be altered so that both teachers and principals act as *facilitators* of human growth.

We have tried to emphasize how leaders can help others develop an openness to experience where individuals are more open and sensitive to data around them. Leaders who develop openness to experience in others provide a safe, nonthreatening environment where creativity and risk-taking flourish and coercive practices are nonexistent. Today's teachers and principals are assuming new professional roles as facilitators, inquirers, reflective practitioners, and human developers. In so doing, they emphasize and practice cooperative engagement and a spirit of collaboration. As teachers and principals assume these new roles, it is much more likely that meaningful relationships and a sense of belonging will permeate the school environment. It also is probable that students will become more responsible for their own learning and moral development.

A Sense of Belonging

A large part of developing self-concept and openness to experience relates to feelings of intimacy and belonging that we all desire. When we identify with others, we are better able to express deep feelings of sensitivity toward others' attitudes and feelings. For many years, perceptual psychologists have described what happens when we have a feeling of identification with others. We are likely to work more harmoniously with them, demonstrate a higher degree of trust, and possess a real extension of ourselves to include others.

Belonging and Students

It is not uncommon to walk through the halls of large high schools boasting enrollments of more than 2,000 students and observe the looks of alienation, disillusionment, and frustration on the faces of many students. Much has been written recently concerning the apparent disconnectedness of students, especially secondary students. As the decades have passed, educational systems have established more and more practices, such as increasing school size, that actually enhance alienation and hinder feelings of belonging and identification with others.

These enormous, highly structured, and cold environments are largely void of caring and personalized attention. Bureaucratic and impersonal, these schools are unable to respond to the needs of many students. The typical U.S. high school has grown so large that many students and teachers believe it has become a difficult institution for people to identify with. Many teachers have 130 students per day, the student-counselor ratio is 500 to 1, and the student-administrator ratio is 600 to 1. A few students—those who fit in—receive personal attention from coaches or other staff members. All too often, though, students are left to fend for themselves, unable to form close connections with adults. Dysfunction, alienation, and even suicide result from the lack of connections and intimacy with others.

Personalization. Ted Sizer, founder of the Coalition of Essential Schools, says that "personalization is the single most important factor that keeps kids in school" (cited in Shore, 1995, p. 76). According to the Carnegie Council for Adolescent Development (1989), finding ways for adults and students to develop personalized relationships in schools is important:

> The student should, on entering middle grade school, join a small community in which people, students and adults, get to know each other well to create a climate for intellectual development. Students should feel that they are part of a community of shared educational purpose. . . . Every student needs at least one thoughtful adult who has the time and takes the trouble to talk with the student about academic matters, personal problems, and the importance of performing well in school (p. 37).

School Size. Fortunately, some schools are developing more personalized learning environments for students, thus enhancing their feelings of identification with others. For example, the New York City School System has created 50 smaller, more personalized high schools. These new schools have been organized according to Coalition of Essential Schools principles, and they emphasize personalization of teaching and learning and close connections between families and schools. Other high schools around the United States are experimenting with reducing school size to create more personalized and meaningful relationships in the school. Though cost factors make it difficult to reorganize large high schools into several separate schools, some districts are experimenting with "schools within schools" or "academic houses." In these models, groups of students are placed with teams of teachers so that smaller groups of teachers, students, and counselors work together, thus individualizing and personalizing the environment.

Advisory Programs. Advisor-advisee programs are another way to enhance belonging in school. There are many different models of these programs, especially at the middle school level. These programs attempt to create more personalized interactions between school staff and students, and they focus on issues such as academic progress, assessment, and community service.

Use of Time. The way time is used in schools often inhibits the development of personalized relationships. Instead of 55-minute class periods, instructional time can be reorganized to allow students and teachers to interact for longer periods. One popular arrangement is block scheduling. Although there are a variety of approaches to block scheduling, the typical pattern is to institute three or four 90- to 120-minute instructional blocks. In some cases, blocks are scheduled daily, while other blocks continue for shorter time periods.

Belonging is also enhanced when teams of teachers work with groups of students for multiple years. This has several benefits. First, there is more time for instruction because teachers do not have to spend the first six weeks of school trying to find out about student abilities. Second, teachers are better able to ascertain how a student has progressed over a period of two to three years rather than one year. Third, curriculum and instruction are geared to individual students rather than a particular grade level. Finally, staying with students for several years naturally leads to closer interpersonal relationships between and among students and teachers—and families.

Belonging and Teachers

In many cases, teachers share the same feelings of alienation in schools that students do. Teacher isolation has permeated schools for decades. Teachers work in their individual classrooms with little time to interact and connect with other adults.

School leaders are in a position to alter the school organization to foster collaboration and a sense of belonging for teachers. Modeling collegiality, initiating collaborative action research, and developing mentoring systems and support networks often heighten feelings of belonging among adults in the school.

Collegiality. According to Judith Warren Little (1982), an expert on collegiality, several types of teacher interactions define collegiality. When teachers observe one another and provide meaningful feedback, they enhance school collegiality. When teachers jointly develop and share teaching materials, they amplify school collaboration. Through these interactions, teachers engender a shared language about teaching and engage in deep and meaningful conversations about teaching and learning.

As facilitators of growth, school leaders can devise structures where more teacher interaction and collaboration occur. For example, principals can assure teachers common planning times to facilitate team teaching. Or principals can develop creative ways for teachers to have the time to dialogue with one another. Making staff meetings participative, open, collaborative, and centered on broad issues of teaching and learning is another way principals can reinforce collegiality and collaboration among staff.

Collaborative Research. Collaborative action research projects can also enhance inquiry and collaboration among staff. Collaborative action research consists of teams of teachers working together on projects designed to find out possible explanations for important questions related to teaching and learning. Teachers who have experience with collaborative research often indicate that their attitude about research improves, collegiality increases, self-esteem is enhanced, and they are more reflective about their practice (Bennett, 1993). However, wise leaders will approach this process cautiously, since many teachers are afraid of research. Administrators can encourage teachers to initiate projects in as nonthreatening a manner as possible, helping dispel the notion that research is so difficult that only university professors can engage in it.

Mentoring. It is no secret that teaching presents many psychological demands that enhance feelings of alienation in the work environment. Working with large numbers of students creates emotional wear and tear. Leaders can improve the personal well-being of teach-ers by helping them develop more positive attitudes about them-selves. Mentoring systems and support networks have the potential to address the emotional stress that often accompanies teaching. These programs can also enhance teachers' feelings of belonging with others.

Many principals have initiated mentoring systems, especially to assist new teachers in becoming socialized in their new roles. Not only do mentoring arrangements orient teachers to district or school norms, but they also offer a personalized support system and can play a role in enhancing self-concept. More experienced teachers who serve as mentors also receive the benefits of being "stretched" profes-sionally. They learn new ideas and practices from novice teachers. Serving in mentor roles also may enhance teachers' sensitivity toward the needs of others.

℞ ℞ ℞

School leaders have the responsibility to develop the self in others with whom they work. This requires a deep understanding of human motivation, as well as an understanding of one's own beliefs about people. It is impossible for leaders to develop the self of others if they have negative views about human nature. Research on effec-tive helpers clearly points to the need for leaders to perceive others as able, worthy, acceptable, and dependable.

In this chapter we have tried to bring attention to how self-concept affects motivation and how beliefs about people affect the teaching and learning process. We have seen many examples of controlling and coercive behavior in schools that demonstrate nega-tive assumptions about people. Grading systems, evaluation models, discipline strategies, and other policies often signify pessimistic views of people.

We also have attempted to emphasize why it is important for leaders to work with people to cultivate openness to experience and a sense of identification with others. There are many ways to do this. Dialogue, collaboration, and creative thinking have the potential to modify the school culture so that people are open to their experiences, are sensitive to other people, and are sensitive to their own reactions to experiences as well.

Most of us want to feel wanted and to feel a sense of identification with others. Sadly, many people in our society are severely lacking in these feelings and experiences. Perhaps the most unfortunate part of this is that many children are growing up without feeling strong identification with others. They lack these experiences at home, in school, and within the community. Educators have the responsibility to devise creative arrangements in schools so that closeness and belonging are enhanced.

It is quite a task for leaders to foster a sense of belonging in the school community. It takes lots of dialogue, thinking, trust, and guts to ensure the positive development of human beings. For many adults and children, home is where we live at night and school is where we live during the day. Why not make school as loving, intimate, and caring as a home should be?

III

LEADERS AND ORGANIZATIONS

CREATING AND RESPONDING TO PURPOSE

PEOPLE ALWAYS ACT IN TERMS OF THE PURPOSES THEY ARE trying to fulfill. Even when others view a person's behavior as completely inappropriate, that individual is behaving in a way that seems right at the time. A burst of anger may confuse observers, but it makes perfect sense to the angry person. Later, that same person may regret the outburst; but at the moment, the behavior seemed purposeful, appropriate, or at least a fitting way to fulfill a pressing need.

Leaders are no exception to this kind of purposeful behavior. They behave in ways they deem appropriate, authentic, and effective at the moment. They attempt to realize a certain purpose or purposes. Our search for a new way to conceive the leadership of schools continues, therefore, with an examination of what effective leaders need to know about their own and others' purposes.

Broad Purposes for School Leadership

In Chapter 1, we reviewed research demonstrating that people who have broad and freeing purposes make better helpers than those who limit their behavior to narrow and, therefore, restricting purposes. This characteristic of how one views purposes is particularly important in a discussion of school leadership.

As we discussed in Chapter 2, the relentless avalanche of daily school activities and the vast scope of principals' domains often drags them into the muck of mundane, management-type issues. You know how the day goes: a sick teacher, a fight on the playground, a broken steamer in the cafeteria, a stolen backpack, a bus breakdown, a rainstorm forcing the cancellation of a baseball game. The unceasing demands and details of an organization trying to meet the educational and social needs of hundreds of students daily are enough to keep anyone sprinting.

In the midst of this chaotic and diverse climate, effective school leaders search within themselves to find the "why" of their own and others' work. Without a broad purpose to guide this work, they find themselves grinding out responses to daily encounters *without* any sense of integration or meaning. Effective leaders put aside the unrelenting particulars of their daily work on occasion to reflect on the major purposes that have brought them to where they are: Why is it that these particular adults in this particular setting gather every weekday with children and young adults? What exactly is the education of children supposed to be about? What is important and unimportant? The broader the scope of the principal's answers to these kinds of questions, the more likely that principal is going to be effective.

For example, without a broad view of the meaning of curriculum, principals may fold under the pressure of parental demands and state mandates for standardized assessment of only basic skills and knowledge in preordained content areas. School leaders probably will need to assess students in these areas to obey state law, abide by board policy, and measure how well children are achieving basic skills. They do not, however, have to assume that this type of assessment is *all* that is important in the curriculum. In fact, they do not even have to assume it is the most important knowledge to assess.

If principals have a narrow view of the purpose of school, then assessing only content knowledge and skills makes sense. This type of leader probably believes that children are in school to learn skills and receive information in adult-defined content areas within adult-centered and adult-controlled classrooms. The teacher is the dispenser of information; the student is the receiver of that information. On the other hand, if principals perceive that the school's purpose is to create healthy, self-regulated, knowledgeable students who can articulate the meaning of what they are doing, then assessment of basic skills becomes only one way to measure success. These principals will attempt to create schools where students show competence in a variety of areas through integrated learning experiences and demonstrations of genuine performance.

Of course, basic skills are important. They serve as the foundation for advanced thinking and conceptualization. But in a school characterized by broad purpose, they are one part of an overall picture, not separate, finite pieces of information that will be discarded after an exam. They are parts of an integrated knowledge system that does not adhere to the rigid compartmentalizing that some schools give it.

Students and Purpose

If a school leader believes that the purpose of education is to offer a broad range of learning activities that encompass many areas of knowledge, all of which are integrated, that leader's school is going to look quite different from a school whose principal believes that the purpose of education is to disseminate enough information to enough students so that their test scores will reach expected standards. What purpose would self-directed learning experiences serve in a school where narrowly conceived content standards guide the curriculum?

None. What purpose would there be to interdisciplinary studies units, community service activities, athletic teams, trips to glean the migrant fields, advisor groups, working in the cafeteria to help serve lunch, designing a cleanup campaign for the school, or planning a dance for new high school students? Mostly none.

Typical assessments of basic skills do not measure other significant student learning that is equally important:

- Students' commitment to others through service activities.
- Students' abilities to enhance the work and outcome of a team.
- Students' knowledge of their own purposes and goals.
- Students' abilities to plan and to act on those plans.
- Students' abilities to direct their own learning activities and to monitor their successes and failures.

Yet it is this kind of learning that requires students to construct personal meaning from their skills and knowledge. This kind of learning requires students not only to gather information and knowledge but to process it. These are the learning experiences that characterize broad, not narrow, purposes.

Broad purposes allow for broad vision and a mission that incorporates all possibilities and potentials for learning. Effective leaders help a school come to consensus on a mission to drive the school's activities. The leader provides myriad opportunities, both formal and informal, for teachers, students, parents, and community members to examine how the school is meeting its common mission.

It is easy for a school to get caught up in its routines and become a victim of its own activities. Soon, the activities become ends in themselves, rather than the means to broader ends. The curriculum also becomes an end, rather than one way of reaching a desired outcome. Instruction becomes an end, rather than one strategy of working toward a vision. Assessment begins to drive the school's activities; it is no longer one tool of many to measure aspirations.

To further examine the concept of broad purposes, consider the following faculty meeting. Middle school teachers are debating whether to continue the outdoor education program for the next year.

Jane: Personally, I don't think it's worth the time we put into planning this trip because we can't get the parents interested enough to even help chaperone. Besides, they never know what to do when anything happens even when they do come. They turn out to be as much of a problem as the kids. Remember Ralph and his dad when they got into that screaming battle at dinner that one night?

Elaine: I agree with Jane. I'm tired of dealing with all the you-know-what that goes on. Pillow fights, beer sneaked in, flat tires—you name it! None of it has anything to do with education. It's a week's vacation for the kids, that's all. I think we should keep the kids here and do something more worthwhile. And when those kids stole that stuff from the store, that was it. I've had it.

John: True, but all the kids really learned a lot from all those experiences. Remember how the kids had to talk to the group about what they had done and apologize for ruining the sense of community we had talked about creating? And remember the trail we found when we were waiting for the tire to be fixed, and the new bird that Sarah identified for her bird book?

Mike: Maybe you've got a point, John, but is it worth the hassle? I'm tired of collecting money and having the buses fouled up.

Tara: Don't the kids always rank this as one of their favorite memories of middle school? I thought I heard someone say that in our first faculty meeting this year.

Tim: Yeah, but they don't have to be responsible for anything.

May: Well, maybe we ought to look at ways to give more responsibility to the kids so that we don't have to do it all.

Alice: Are you kidding? Why would we want to give the kids more responsibility when they already screw up more than they should? That sounds stupid to me.

May: I was only trying to point out that there might be other ways to look at doing things than the way we're looking at them right now.

Mike: Easy for you to say, May. You're new here. What if you'd been doing this for five years like I have? Then you'd think differently.

May: Well, maybe, but I think. . . .

Tim (interrupting): It's just not realistic to think of getting the kids to be more responsible for this thing. They can barely remember to bring their notes from home saying they can go. I had to call three parents myself because kids forgot their notes.

John: Aren't we forgetting about why we created this week to begin with?

Elaine: John, you can forget your philosophizing just once. The fact is that too many things go wrong every year. I vote for putting an end to this nonsense and getting back to school stuff for the week. Besides, testing starts in two weeks, and the kids are still wild. I don't know how well they will score when we've completely forgotten school for a week.

Jane: Now you're talking. I vote with Elaine. Let's come to our senses here and forget this week. We have enough to do.

Tara: But what about the kids?

Jane: What about them?

Mike: Maybe we should keep it. After all, it has sort of become a tradition around here. I don't want every kid mad at me because I voted to do away with it. They always find out how everyone thinks.

May: But aren't there good reasons. . . .

Mike (interrupting): I guess if I weren't the only one who voted that way, it would be okay. *[He turns to Jane and Elaine.]* Are you two really going to vote against it?

Jane and Elaine (in unison): Yes!

John: Since when are we even voting? I don't remember voting on anything before.

Elaine: That's because your head is always on another planet, John. *[Several people laugh; John looks annoyed.]*

Jane: Well, is it settled then? It's almost time for classes to start. *[Most people nod their heads yes, although May and Tara look at the floor. John stares pensively out the window.]*

How did this middle school faculty do at discussing purpose? Clearly, some people wanted to bring the focus back to the purpose of the outdoor education week. John, who seems to have a reputation for asking philosophical questions, raises the issue of purpose several times. He points out some of the advantages that the near disasters have created for kids' learning. May, a new teacher, also tries to raise some consciousness about the purpose of the trip, but she is silenced with interruptions and snide remarks. Tara attempts to talk about what the week means to the kids, but no one wants to listen.

Basically, fatigue wins in the end. People are tired of dealing with all the details of the trip and the challenging behavior of a few students. The teachers who seem to have more authority fail to see the opportunity this activity offers to teach planning and responsibility skills. They also don't see that disaster and failure can create teachable moments for the whole group. The voices of purpose get drowned out in the noise of those who are wearied by the effort the week requires or disappointed in students' behavior. They have forgotten to step back and try to remember why the week was created in the first place. Then they could work on ways to remedy some of the difficult parts.

Sometimes we are inclined just to do away with things that are hard; we don't hang in with something that has a sound purpose in order to work through problems. But when leaders "correct for drift," that is what they do. They remind everyone of the "why" of the event so that they can get grounded in purpose again. Then they help figure out ways to turn the negative parts of the event into positive learning experiences. The faculty members in the previous meeting scenario were not in the frame of mind to "correct for drift." They didn't listen to those who tried to bring the discussion back to the purpose of the activity, and the outdoor education program may be dropped from the curriculum.

Purpose in Open and Closed Systems

When means to ends begin to look like ends, the school has become a closed system. It has become a place where assumptions are no longer challenged, where ends are evaluated without consideration for whether they should even be the ends. External and internal feedback gets put into the loop, but the loop is flawed. Nowhere in the loop is there a place to examine purpose instead of results. This type of closed system reinforces narrow purposes and narrow vision. It is a system that makes it easy to plan, implement, and evaluate activities without searching for their meaning.

Open systems, on the other hand, are characterized by broad purposes and broad sweeps of activity that are difficult to plan for, implement, and evaluate. By nature they are elusive and constantly forming and reforming. They flow where discovery takes them, sometimes becoming circuitous and seemingly random. From the underlying purpose driving the activities, however, a purposeful pattern eventually emerges, possibly one that was unknown before.

An effective leader monitors the school system for its openness and flexibility. A leader who is purposeful and driven by vision is a navigator for the system, correcting for drift. These leaders seek the collective conscience of the school and then guard it in their everyday activities (as the next section shows). They expect others to be guardians of the collective conscience, too, so they spend time teaching about it and asking questions of others when it appears that the conscience has been set aside. Effective school leaders are the people who ask *why* things are being done as well as *what* is being done. They hold up each activity of the school against a standard of collective vision and agreement. They ask what things mean, why things happen a certain way, and whether the meaning and purpose of an activity are what the school agreed to support. They also guide staff members to live out the vision, values, and collective conscience.

Effective leaders see the broad landscape, and they remind people that there are many diverse paths to reach a broad goal. The more paths that everyone sees and agrees to, the greater the chance the school will meet the purposes of all students. But each path must lead to the horizon. Policies, practices, procedures, curriculum, instruction, activities, and materials all must lead students to a future where they will become self-directed, competent, healthy adults.

Seeking a Freeing Purpose

The purposes of schools and their leaders also must free people to seek their highest potential. They must allow individuals to become all they dream of being. If the leader believes that his or her purpose is to control and manipulate others' purposes, the system breaks down. If the leader must control everything, then no matter how broadly stated the mission, it still is the mission of only one person, not a collective vision. Just as leaders exhort teachers to free students to search for personal meaning in their studies and learning experiences, so must leaders free teachers to search for personal meaning in their work.

The work of all adults in the school must be guided by a common vision of why the school exists in the first place. This clear rationale must be shared, and it must be broad enough to encompass almost endless ways of realizing the purpose. These reasons for existence will be the foundation of everyone's work, and they will create their own patterns of organization and rationality if they are allowed to emerge. These purposes will allow individuals to pursue—freely and with encouragement—any path that seems to support the purposes. The paths will vary with the individual interpretations and talents of the faculty. No one method, no one strategy, no one textbook, no one way of doing things will work for everyone. Yet the guiding principles will belong to the whole school. They will be the standards by which all faculty and staff will judge their work and student performance.

For example, if a school agrees that greater understanding about, appreciation for, and respect of different cultures is an underlying purpose of the school, then this purpose will guide a school leader's response to difficult situations like the one in the following scenario.

> Two student leaders have requested a meeting with the principal. The president of the student council and the chair of the student activities committee want to talk about Homecoming activities. Because Homecoming occurs so close to the beginning of the school year, the week is always fraught with tension and anxiety as students overextend

their commitments. They become exhausted and get a bit snippy toward each other and adults. The principal, Mr. Howard, knows this phenomenon well, so he is on alert to be particularly supportive of these student leaders this week.

Cheryl, the president, begins the meeting. She wants to know if Mr. Howard will approve one of the student council's fund-raising activities: a slave auction. She didn't think there would be any problem with it, but the student council advisor thought it would be best if she and Chad, the activities chair, cleared everything with the principal "just in case."

Chad chimes in with a description of all the plans for the event. He gives Mr. Howard a handout showing how the event will proceed, where and when it will occur, and what revenue it likely will generate for the student council. They are desperate to raise funds because they have to share the revenue from concession sales at football games with the middle school this year, and they are operating on a tight budget. The slave auction has always been well attended and lots of fun for students as they auction off personal services to the highest bidder.

Mr. Howard sees that the event has been well planned. He also sees the weary faces of the two students who have put so much of their personal energy into the plans. He asks Cheryl and Chad if they have shared the plans with the entire council. They have, and everyone thinks it is a good idea. He asks them if they anticipate any problems. Cheryl hesitates before responding.

"Well, we know that a slave auction might offend some of the African American students, so we changed it to a personal services auction for that reason. Also, I asked Dennis [a well-known and respected African American student leader and athlete] if he would be offended by the auction. He said no. So we figure that it's probably okay with everybody."

Mr. Howard sighs. He does not believe that the students should go ahead with the auction because no matter what name is given to the event, it still represents the selling of a person to be a slave to another, and he believes this tradition is a very sorry page in U.S. history. He looks away for a minute, trying to collect his thoughts.

How can he support the students yet help them realize the ugly symbolism of the auction? He doesn't have time personally to work with them to create a new event. He knows that they already have worked hard and will be upset and probably even angry that he won't approve the auction. Then when they report back to the council, all the students will be angry. He wishes that their advisor had taken more of a leadership role and seized this opportunity to teach about cultural awareness and respect before the planning went this far.

Finally, Mr. Howard turns back to the expectant students. He tells them up front that he can't support the auction. Their faces fall, then harden. He explains his personal feelings and concerns about why it is important not to recreate in the school such an ugly page of history. He talks with them about the position that Cheryl put Dennis in when she asked him if he would be offended by the auction. He tries to get them to see that hardly any high school student would say that he or she was offended because it would take tremendous personal courage to buck a long-standing tradition—especially in light of the fact that there are very few African American students in the school.

Mr. Howard realizes that he is getting nowhere fast with the two students, so he cuts short his comments. He tells them how sorry he is that he can't support them since they obviously have put much time and effort into planning the event. He offers to come to the student council to explain his reasons if Cheryl and Chad would like him to. They shake their heads no, and leave, obviously distraught. Mr. Howard wishes them good luck and makes a mental note to see them both later, once the stress of the next week is over and things are calmer.

Next he heads out to find the student council advisor to explain what just happened. He wants to explain his reasoning firsthand. The advisor listens to Mr. Howard's reasons for saying no, but disagrees with him. He also says he wishes that Mr. Howard had told him all of this before the year started. Mr. Howard apologizes and says he hadn't really thought about it until the students came in.

After leaving the advisor, Mr. Howard takes a long walk outside the building to think about what just happened. He feels more than a little irritated by the teacher's response, and he's a bit discouraged that his voice seems to be the only one questioning the morality of the endeavor. He cools off, heads back to his office, and adds an item to the agenda for the next faculty meeting. He also writes himself a note: Remind everybody of our commitment to cultural respect and understanding. He then grabs his sandwich and heads for the cafeteria knowing that word will get around fast about his disapproval. He hopes he can head off disaster by informally talking to people at lunch.

This school leader faced a knotty issue that challenged his goal to be supportive of student leadership. But he decided that the purpose of the school, which included understanding and respect for diverse cultures, was more important this time than supporting the students. Mr. Howard believed that in the long run his decision was more supportive of the students than allowing them to go ahead with the auction. But he also knew that it would be hard to convince the students and faculty of that. Still, Mr. Howard believed it was important to remind the students and staff members of their commitment to understanding, appreciating, and respecting diverse cultures; and he decided not to fold under the enormous pressure he felt to go ahead with the students' plan.

By standing up for the shared purpose of the school, this leader faced opposition but still guarded the collective conscience of the school. He helped teach an important lesson about following through on beliefs and values in every school activity.

Dialogue and Purpose

Schools that adopt broad and freeing purposes are characterized by dialogue that includes everyone who has a stake in the school's mission. This dialogue is frequent, and it encompasses big issues, not small ones. People talk about ways to accomplish the mission, not about parking or the copy machine. All people are expected to add their voices to the conversations, to contribute to the overall learning of the organization, to dissent when necessary, and to help bring resolution to difficult problems. The adult interactions, therefore, are directed toward a broad school mission and toward strategies that foster greater student growth.

Schools that are characterized by broad purpose also create ways for students to participate in the dialogue. Children as young as five can understand why they are doing things and what teachers hope to help them learn. Even kindergartners can help decide on and plan for activities that will enrich their learning. In doing so, they learn skills through authentic action rather than a contrived situation. But they will understand these concepts only if teachers expect that kind of behavior in the classroom and create opportunities for it to occur. Students learn very early that teachers and other adults expect them to question, to seek solutions, to learn where and how to gather information, to experiment with a variety of responses, to help others seek information, and to report to others on their learning.

In their earliest interactions with students, teachers can begin to develop their roles as facilitators rather than answer-givers. They can help students learn to process the myriad facts and information that they garner through their research, activity, and experimentation. It is in these student-teacher interactions that students begin to understand broad purpose and meaning in learning. It is where the foundation for self-directed learning is built. Schools driven by broad and freeing purposes are characterized by group conversations with students, one-on-one conversations with students, and planning with students. This dialogue is filled with not only the *what* and *how* of activities, but the *why*.

Leaders in schools with broad purpose facilitate a climate where students have opportunities to examine their purposes. Educators encourage students to learn research and technology skills so that they have access to the widest, broadest, and deepest thinking in the world on topics with which they are most involved. Teachers encourage students to find personal meaning in their academic learning; and teachers assist students in finding ways to put into action the kinds of thinking and changes that are happening within them. Students experience purpose and meaning through many avenues: classroom activities, community experiences, extracurricular activities, service activities, apprenticeships, internships, leadership and governance within the school, and connections with other students in other schools.

A school that fosters broad and freeing purposes for students emphasizes connections and interrelationships, personal responsibility, concern and care for others, curiosity *and* tentativeness, truth seeking, and enthusiasm. This kind of school values difference and diversity, but it also honors the connectedness and community of all living things. Leaders in such a school constantly ask people, "Why?" Then leaders do everything in their power to find a way to make things happen when the answers begin sounding like the following:

- Because it is the right thing to do.
- Because it is our responsibility as a community.
- Because we will learn more if we do it this way.
- Because we need to support each other.
- Because these people need our help.
- Because we can get more information if we go.
- Because she knows more than we do, and we need to talk to her.
- Because they are trying something we've been thinking about doing, and we need to see how it's working.

These kinds of responses demonstrate that people are filled with purpose, and their purposes are all-encompassing and empowering, not narrow and self-serving.

Purpose in the Community

Effective school leaders also address the purposes of other adults who work with students or who interact with the school in some way. They create a climate that allows teachers to examine the purposes and meaning of their behavior as they work with students and within the school community. Because schools are public agencies, many people in the community believe a piece of the school belongs to them. The tradition of tax-supported schools under the local control of elected officials means that principals and other leaders must be aware of the purposes of many people who are outside the daily realm of the school. Their thinking influences decisions, regulations, and policies that govern the school. Person-centered school leaders cannot ignore the political arena within which schools flourish—or flounder.

Especially in an era when people are challenging all government entities, when student performance seems lackluster despite increased expenditures, and when special interest groups have gained greater power, leaders must be vigilant about the purposes of people who interact with the schools. The principal, in particular, must guard judiciously yet vigorously the best interests of students. The principal also must interpret the mission and vision of the school for these external interests. This guardianship is crucial in maintaining the purpose of schooling and in curbing community passivity about schools. Passivity sometimes allows special interest groups to gain control of the school. Often they then make sweeping changes that enhance their own narrow purposes but stamp out the broad purposes essential for students to learn and teachers to teach.

Effective leaders identify community and parent leaders who believe in the broad purpose of the school and who can articulate its mission and vision to the community in a variety of forums that are beyond the principal's scope. Effective leaders go a long way toward increasing community support when they integrate well-informed, supportive community and parent leaders into the daily operation of the school. These stakeholders can interpret the school to the wider community, and they act as a buffer for those whose purposes may be self-serving rather than student-serving. Even if there are no external challenges to the school's purpose, these leaders still serve as important links to the community.

The Bensenville, Illinois, New American Schools Project is a fascinating example of the importance of knowing and responding to the purposes of others who have a stake in the school. In a historical treatise on a hugely unsuccessful reform effort, Mirel (1994) highlights the disaster that befell the Bensenville school district after it received more than $1 million from the New American Schools

Development Corporation in 1992. The goal was to completely reform the district schools around entirely new purposes and vision. Here is the Bensenville story:

> The vision of the Bensenville project was a "break-the-mold" (Mirel, 1994, p. 489) school. It rested on the belief that the community should serve as the school, not just the school building; that learning should be thought of as lifelong, not just a K–12 proposition; and that what was happening in the schools at the time had to be completely revised (Mirel, 1994). Part of the vision included the following:

> - Using adults other than certified teachers to offer instruction to students.
> - Developing community learning sites where students would spend time in academic pursuits, observing and participating in real-life events.
> - Keeping the schools and other learning sites open and available seven days a week from early in the morning to late at night.
> - Developing a yearlong school program.
> - Focusing on instruction individualized to each student's needs and assisted by technology.
> - Assessing learning through performance, portfolios, and projects rather than through grades in content areas.
> - Organizing students in nongraded, multi-aged groups of learners rather than in more traditional age-defined groups.
> - Governing the school through a team not elected by the local tax district but selected from a broad-based representation of community members who expressed interest in moving forward with the reform movement.

Clearly, this school district examined its past purposes and vision, found fault with their outcomes, and created a new paradigm to replace the old. This paradigm was founded on very different principles of participatory governance, student-directed learning, community-based leaning opportunities, and instructors as facilitators and supporters of individual learning. It was an exciting time and an exciting idea. The reform movement fell flat, however, despite initial support from almost every important constituent group.

What happened? The idea of purpose reared its head. Many of the adults who originally supported the project began to experience how the schools' new purposes would challenge their own individual purposes or the purposes of the groups to which they belonged and felt allegiance. For example, one high school began to see how the new configuration could result in a more even distribution of monies in the district. Their school would no longer be the "rich" school and the other the "poor" one. Also, as students spread themselves throughout the community, the distribution of minority students would change, and all high school students would interact with all others. This change would significantly influence how many minority students would interact with students from the high school unused to ethnic diversity.

In addition, the teachers' union began to fight the notion that noncertified adults could teach students effectively. Teachers in the wealthier high school saw that salaries might have to be evened out, and they might lose some of their salaries as the wages of teachers in the poorer district were brought into alignment.

In terms of governance, school board members began to see how their decision- and policy-making powers might be challenged by a wider group of community members interested in education reform. They demanded clearer delineation of authority and eventually balked at supporting the changes.

In the end, the school district did not get continued support from the New American Schools Development Corporation. What was once a dream—worked on and supported by a broad-based coalition of people interested in reinventing the purpose and vision of their schools—became a nightmare. As the purposes of the newly conceived schooling process began to challenge traditional reasons for and ways of doing things, the process got ugly. Self-serving purposes—and purposes of control and power—won out over what seemed to be purposes that would result in a better education for all children in the community.

When push came to shove, cooperation, collaboration, and agreement turned out to be superficial consensus. Resistance to reform became so strong that no one could overcome it, not even the visionaries who originally designed what appeared to be a powerful educational plan.

As the Bensenville story illustrates, purpose is serious business. It takes long, arduous, difficult, complex, and frustrating dialogue to review and understand purpose and vision. It takes truth seeking and truth telling that is not customary in schools. It takes excruciating honesty from everyone, and it takes willingness to set aside personal agendas in favor of a broad, more encompassing vision and purpose that embraces and frees individuals to pursue teaching and learning in a variety of ways.

The Leader's Individual Purpose

To help others grow in their own purposes, leaders clearly must know and believe in the purposes that guide their own actions. These purposes allow them to act consistently in the best interests of students and the school. Such clarity requires that principals and other school leaders reflect on and decide about what is most important. Not everything can have equal importance, or else nothing will receive quality time and attention.

As we showed in Chapter 2, principals are quickly swamped by the endless minutiae of leading a school, so setting priorities is essential to a leader's success. These priorities must emerge from the purposes that leaders see in their actions and their work. Others also will note what the priorities say about the leader's purposes. Leaders cannot escape two facts:

1. They must set priorities. If they don't, nothing will ever get done.
2. Whatever priorities they set will be scrutinized by stakeholders in the school. These stakeholders will then draw conclusions about the purpose of their own work.

Formally or informally, others in the school community talk about what the leader does, and they take guidance from these actions for their own activities. Because people draw conclusions about their purposes no matter what, good leaders seize this opportunity to clarify their own purposes. Clarifying purpose is a never-ending process, and it is one of the most important things that school leaders do.

Effective leaders who bring a broad and altruistic purpose to their work face an interesting dilemma: the feeling that they are so important to the school that they cannot give up anything to others. Because schools have such ethical and momentous purposes, most leaders experience their work as consequential and significant. For example, leading a school makes principals feel needed. Something portentous always awaits the principal's attention; frequently, it is something that allows a principal to make someone's life better. There is a dangerous seductiveness to this.

Principals can be enticed into believing that because people need them, they must control everything and do everything. When principals begin to seize control of everything, the school turns into a dependent organization, even if the principal's motives are generous and other-serving. The school becomes a place that reflects one person who is totally committed, but it is not a place that reflects a collective endeavor.

Truly effective principals help others gain greater insight, competence, and confidence; take more risks; and depend more on their own instincts and perceptions. As the school becomes more broadly purposeful and more freeing, the principal will begin to feel some disappointment at being needed less. Actually, the principal is still needed as much, just in a different way. The principal now acts as a rudder, navigating people around the inevitable shoals, reminding people of the broader horizon, and preventing them from drowning in the narrower wakes that always beckon.

Another unusual dilemma that arises among purposeful leaders is the "ennui" factor. For example, when principals first begin their jobs, they are filled with high expectations, but they're also a bit inexperienced in the ways of the administrative life. Soon they become more skilled and capable. They begin to have higher expectations for themselves and others. This phenomenon repeats itself until finally one day the principal looks around and realizes that there is nothing more he or she wants to achieve or accomplish. Any higher achievement would be completely unrealistic. Beginning again each year becomes tedious and unfulfilling.

This syndrome happens to the best of leaders. In fact, it probably happens only to the very best of leaders. They have given so much, accomplished so much, and committed so much of their lives to this meaningful work that there seems to be nothing left to do except to begin again. Their spirit seeks the challenge of doing something altogether different. At this juncture, leaders must take stock of their situations and make personal and professional decisions about whether to stay or to seek some other equally fulfilling work. It is difficult to find work as important as leading schools, so principals may have to struggle for some time regarding what to do with the skills and competencies they have gained over many years of successful leadership.

❧ ❧ ❧

The climate of school leadership does not lend itself easily to an examination of purpose. Good leaders, however, make purpose a priority. They seek every way possible to create a climate that enhances broad and freeing purpose in others. These leaders are challenged on a regular basis by people who forget that activities, events, and curriculum are not ends in themselves. They are the means to ends. Creation of broad purposes that underlie all the school's activities results in meaningful dialogue, wide participation from all stakeholders, and a sense of direction to guide every person's actions. Broad purpose that is shared throughout the school also lessens the chance that special interest groups will take over the school's agenda.

The kind of leadership that purposeful action requires can create problematic situations for leaders. Leaders who create purposeful schools are themselves purposeful and committed to others. They must be vigilant not to create a school where their vision becomes the only vision. They must be wary of the seductiveness that comes with helping to build a collective conscience, making certain that the conscience truly is collective. They also must be prepared to face professional burnout when their work over many years finally creates the kind of enriching organization they have always desired. When it appears that no more can be done, it is time for the school leader to seek other avenues for professional fulfillment.

Clarifying purpose is one of the most important jobs that a school leader tackles. Setting priorities based on clear and shared purposes is vital. It makes the school leader guardian of the school's collective conscience, and it enables all in the school community to seek their own vision within the broader school mission.

AUTHENTICITY AND ORGANIZATIONS

SCHOOL ORGANIZATIONS ARE DYNAMIC ENTITIES WHOSE success or failure depends on participants' interactions. This success or failure is, of course, a function of both the leader and the organization members. An educational leader's achievements largely depend on the quality of these interactions with school personnel.

Even the most well-intentioned leader may be defeated by an uncooperative or hostile organization. Likewise, organizations ready and willing to operate productively may be frustrated and inhibited by an ineffective leader. Effective leaders are professional facilitators skilled at helping organizations and their members achieve fulfillment. How well they accomplish that end is determined in large measure by their personal and professional authenticity.

Being Authentic

In Chapter 1, we noted that research shows good helpers to be authentic. That is, these kinds of leaders are self-revealing, rather than self-concealing. Their behavior is such that people around them can read their attitudes, beliefs, goals, concerns, and expectations. They are predictable.

To be self-revealing does not mean that leaders must share the most intimate aspects of their lives. Authenticity does not require someone to be overemotional. Authenticity, however, demands genuineness, honesty, and willingness to confront the facts. It requires us to be, straightforwardly, who we truly are.

At one time or another, many educators or parents have encountered an administrator who is playing a role, trying to be what he or she is not. We've learned to see through such behavior with relative ease because the leader's deepest beliefs, attitudes, and values rarely can be hidden. Sooner or later, these truths have a way of betraying the owner.

Consider this real-life visit to a new rural high school:

> The proud superintendent was giving a tour of the building. He pointed out to his visitor every physical detail of the shops, cafeteria, bus loading docks, auditorium, and gymnasium. On returning to the superintendent's office, the visitor observed, "It's a beautiful building, George, but you didn't show me a classroom."
>
> "Oh, that's right," the superintendent agreed, and he arranged for a visit.
>
> After an hour's observation, the visitor returned to the superintendent's office just as a bus driver arrived with a small boy in one hand and the broken arm from a bus seat in the other. The driver reported that someone pushed someone else, and the young boy was pushed against the arm of the seat, breaking it. Knowing what this superintendent thought was important, it wasn't hard to predict his reaction. He was furious with the child, and the superintendent behaved as if his own arm had been broken, which, in a symbolic way, was true.

It is hard for leaders to hide what truly motivates them. Motivation shows quite clearly to the people with whom they interact.

We have observed that everyone has empathy, the capacity and skill to infer the nature of other people's attitudes and beliefs. Empathy is especially necessary for leaders who are in the position to help or hinder other people's self-fulfillment. We are all keenly aware of the feelings, attitudes, and beliefs of wives, husbands, lovers, enemies, or leaders with whom we have to work. Accordingly, students, teachers, parents, and staff members are deeply sensitive to the belief systems of those in positions to affect them.

Leaders might be surprised and embarrassed at the depth and accuracy of the perceptions their fellow workers have about them. So long as the leader has any authority to affect the hopes, dreams, and aspirations of people about him or her, those people will be keenly aware of the leader's beliefs, values, and habits. It is a matter of survival for them. It also deeply affects their commitment, motivation, and efficiency in carrying out their tasks.

Nothing is more difficult to deal with than an unpredictable leader. Generally, we cope with a mean or dictatorial leader by setting up defenses, avoiding contact, pretending acquiescence, or finding ingenious ways to escape the leader's field of influence. An unpredictable leader is much more upsetting than a challenging one.

The Leader's Belief System

People behave according to their personal belief systems. A leader's authenticity, therefore, depends on the nature of his or her belief system as well as an ability to share it meaningfully. A trustworthy belief system makes it much easier and safer to be truly authentic. Generally speaking, trustworthy belief systems will have the following characteristics:

• **Comprehensive.** Truly authentic people have a rich store of information and beliefs from which to choose.

• **Realistic.** Belief systems of authentic people are in touch with reality. These leaders can support their beliefs. They do not do things just because "they might work." They have tenable reasons for what they do and the beliefs they hold.

- **Consistent.** Their belief systems are internally consistent; the beliefs they hold fit comfortably together. As a consequence, the behavior they produce is generally trustworthy, with a minimum of contradictions. Others are likely to regard the resulting behavior as confident and assured.

- **Appropriate.** Authentic leaders' belief systems are truly related to the tasks at hand. For example, they avoid applying a manipulation-of-forces theory to working with people, which would be frustrating and unproductive.

- **Adaptable.** Belief systems are not set in concrete. Instead, they are continuously subject to review, and the leader changes them when better or more appropriate information becomes available. A trustworthy belief system can be changed through the incorporation of new information or experience and yet be internally consistent.

Two Kinds of Behavior

Everyone displays two kinds of behavior: coping and expressive (Maslow, 1954). Coping behaviors are the things we do to manage life, to deal with the problems and circumstances with which we are confronted. Each of us also behaves in expressive ways, the things we do almost without thinking that are straightforward outcomes of our feelings, attitudes, and beliefs.

Psychologists tell us that truly healthy personalities do very little coping; just by expressing, they cope. People with belief systems that are comprehensive, realistic, consistent, appropriate, and adaptable do not have to worry much about being authentic. Simply being themselves produces behavior that is on target, consistent, and supportable without having to work at it. Their beliefs also may be expressed with compelling passion. Interacting with authentic people, we come away feeling, "She's really got what it takes!" or "He knows what he's doing!"or "It's good to work with her" or "I feel a lot of trust in him" or "You always know where you stand."

People without trustworthy belief systems behave tentatively. They behave halfway; on-again, off-again, and as though they are unsure. In turn, this gives those who work with them a feeling of insecurity, doubt, uncertainty, and even suspicion about the leader's true motives. People come away feeling, "You just never know!" Even worse, leaders with belief systems that are seriously flawed or limited are likely to feel inadequate and fearful that their colleagues and coworkers will find out their weaknesses. Such feelings may cause the leader to feel personally threatened.

Feelings of threat, as we have seen earlier, produce tunnel vision and self-defense. When leaders retreat to these kinds of defenses, it is likely to result in autocratic behavior or an unwillingness to listen to or consider alternative actions. These feelings also may cut leaders off from coworkers, who have erected psychological barriers to protect themselves. Unfortunately, barriers that keep others out also keep the threatened person in. Thus, threatened leaders may become isolated from the very information and experiences they need to grow and learn.

The Person-Centered Leader

The person-centered organization described in Chapter 3 depends on open communication among all participants, including leaders (Wheatley, 1992). Person-centered organizations require the freest possible flow of information. That flow can be achieved only when participants feel safe enough to tackle relevant problems, drop their usual defenses, and actively engage in the give-and-take of open dialogue. Organizations become more or less effective as the people involved learn to trust one another, drop their defenses, and participate with deeper and deeper levels of personal involvement. Leaders play a critical role in whether such growth occurs.

Like it or not, simply being the designated leader of a school, classroom, or organization carries with it the responsibility for facilitating these processes. Whether groups succeed or fail is strongly influenced by the extent and depth of the leader's own ability to be authentically involved with the processes of the organization. Facilitative leaders can do much to initiate, support, and encourage the transition of an organization's focus, communication, and level of personal commitment. They can help an organization self-destruct or coalesce into an efficient and productive group. Leaders can begin by setting an example of personal authenticity, a willingness to be who they truly are and to share themselves with all group members.

Hazards of Leadership

Being an authentic, facilitative leader is never easy, especially for administrators. The mere fact that you are the administrator raises expectations among organization members. Job descriptions, custom, and tradition all define the leader's position in ways quite different from what the leader may wish. Consequently, leaders find that colleagues are slow to accept them in a new or different role. They may even resist the leader's attempts to change.

This puts the leader who desires to be an authentic member of a group in the ticklish position of having to wear two hats: being the boss, information provider, and assessor on one hand, and being an authentic, participating member on the other. The difficulty of smoothly playing out these two roles can cause the tenderhearted to give up the struggle altogether. Facilitative leaders may have to make repeated efforts to demonstrate that they are sincerely ready to relinquish their designated power and authority when it interferes with the organization's processes.

Leaders who cannot share themselves or do not believe it is appropriate to do so will find it difficult or impossible to create or sustain a person-centered system. Unfortunately, some aspects of administration make it difficult for educational leaders to risk authenticity with their coworkers. For example, being a school principal is much more stressful than many suppose. From an outsider's view-point, a principal is the boss, responsible for everything that occurs in or out of the building. In fact, most decisions are not the principal's, although total accountability may be laid at the principal's door.

Also, being authentic means allowing yourself to be vulnerable to others. Yet principals, for example, operate in a work environment that tends to be filled with conflict, special interests, political maneu-vering, and the pressures from endless demands on time and atten-tion. With all this tension, principals become gun-shy when their words are turned around and used against them or their confidential-ity is broken. A leader must be personally confident and courageous to risk sharing himself or herself openly in a hostile environment.

Some of the most problematic issues leaders face are matters of personnel, and principals are bound to confidentiality. They cannot respond to comments that reflect on the performance of personnel. This prohibition places them in agonizing situations where they are expected to share their knowledge but cannot. Observers not privy to these restrictions can easily jump to the conclusion that the administrator is not being candid or is refusing to engage in dialogue. Thus, they believe the principal must be hiding something, which, of course, is true—but that's an inviolate requirement of the job.

Almost universally, principals complain of the isolation of their positions. They are responsible for their building and its faculty and students, all of whom, at least, have each other to talk to. But the principal has little opportunity to talk with other principals, except on special occasions. That is a lonely place to be. The isolation is further exacerbated by the feeling that it is inappropriate to share deep feelings with teachers in the building because, inevitably, the matters principals would like to talk about involve other people in the same building.

Teachers, fearful of evaluation, can "play things very close to the chest." Right or wrong, that is reality. Peter Senge (1990), in a discussion of organizational "truth telling," points out how difficult it is to create organizations where participants tell the truth. It is difficult to continue being open when others do not respond in similar fashion. Any faculty represents innumerable agendas, some of which the principal may be aware of. Other issues may be totally outside his or her awareness. This can be confusing and even painful for a well-meaning leader, but it, too, is reality.

Though teachers' unions are important for a faculty, even the most liberal unions produce adversarial thinking. Because they see their jobs as protecting teachers, they can and often do exacerbate feelings of "us and them," which makes authenticity difficult for administrators. Such polarization can be carried so far, especially in time of stress, that administrators are regarded as "the enemy."

Fear is another stress endemic in public schools. The whole educational culture is built on right answers. As a consequence, everyone—students, teachers, supervisors, and administrators—fears making mistakes. Mistakes are synonymous with failure, and they must be avoided like the plague. Mistakes are too often regarded as catastrophes or personal failures instead of being accepted as useful information. These attitudes are compounded by evaluation schemes, grading systems, or rewards and punishments of a hundred varieties, all of which hang labels around people's necks: excellent, good, bad, indifferent, failure.

The paranoia arising from fear of mistakes extends to everyone in the system. For example, parents worry about their children's grades. Students treat grades as indicators of personal capacity, acceptance, and worth. Because teachers are constantly involved in evaluation and grading, they are anxious about being evaluated and fear evaluators—not just educational leaders but their fellow teachers. In most schools, including college and graduate schools, it is rare to find teachers interacting with one another, visiting each other's classes, or talking about truly professional concerns. Though teachers work in close proximity, they maintain a careful distance from each other. Observing this state of affairs in a university led one educator to define "academic freedom" as "the professor's right to teach extraordinarily badly without ever being questioned."

Organizations or individuals fearful of mistakes seriously inhibit possibilities for innovation, growth, or change. They contribute to the maintenance of bureaucracies and place roadblocks in the way of much-needed reform. Fearful people want to play it safe (Combs, 1992). Unfortunately, organizations or individuals intent on self-defense and fearful of change make progress or innovation difficult, if not impossible. Change involves risk, and avoiding risk results only in the status quo. In the meantime, the world moves on, and those fearful of risk and mistakes fall further and further behind.

Resistance to Change

Still another barrier to growth and change is the insidious effect of the manipulation-of-forces theory. Our culture is imbued with this way of coping with people and the physical world. Approaching educational leadership from a person-centered frame of reference will require new thinking, planning, and action—and those things are always difficult and awkward at first.

Because they are new and different, these innovations will be approached tentatively and with uncertainty. That almost guarantees that the innovator will make mistakes. It is all too easy then to back off and give up the effort. This would not be so bad if such action were only temporary. What too often happens is this: Innovators are distressed by shaky results. They give up on projects, leaving ideas unfairly tested. For years after, the fearful innovators exclaim, "Try that? No way! We tried that once, and we can tell you it will never work!"

People who have been thinking and behaving in a given way for long periods of time must expect to make mistakes and experience discomfort in new roles. Wise educational leaders understand this and provide courageous innovators freedom, support, and encouragement.

An interesting example of how constraints on innovation and change may affect the entire profession can be found in what happened to the concept of "action research" in U.S. education. In the late 1940s and early 1950s, the idea of "action research" took off in schools all over the country. The idea was that everyone should be involved in educational research, trying something new every year in whatever one's job. The innovation did not have to be world shaking; it was the effort that counted, the involvement in the process.

Whole school systems enlisted in the effort, and hundreds of teachers were caught up in the excitement. Then, the Soviets sent Sputnik into space. The United States was shocked. Americans believed that their scientists were the best in the world, and here they were, beaten by the "enemy." Searching for reasons for this humiliation, the nation decided that a major fault lay in public schools, which did not produce enough scientists. Accordingly, billions of dollars were poured into educational research, regional laboratories, and the invention of a whole new class of "educational research experts" at the doctoral level.

These experts were specialists in research design and high-level statistics. They also were disdainful of action research and teachers, and they made no bones about letting people know it. Unhappily, teachers and administrators came to believe that truly meaningful research could only be done by experts gifted in statistics and research design. To this day, when asked about research, educational leaders and teachers everywhere are likely to reply, "Research? Oh, I don't know how to do that. I don't have statistics or that kind of training." A promising innovation was destroyed by an unfortunate state of mind.

Producing more researchers seemed like a good idea, but no one gave heed to how the effort would be seen by teachers and administrators on the front line where, in the final analysis, the work gets done. In Chapter 1, we spoke of the importance of empathy, being aware of how things seem to others. Failure to do so can, and often does, result in a stalemate wherein, "What you make on the oranges, you lose on the bananas."

Earned and Unearned Authority

Leaders in any system possess two kinds of authority: earned and unearned. Unearned authority is a consequence of credentials, job description, custom, or tradition. It came with the job, though it may have been supported by the leader's hard work. It was not, however, bestowed by the members of the organization.

Depending on their success in becoming accepted by the group, authentic leaders may, in time, be given authority by organization members. This is earned authority, granted to a leader by his or her colleagues on the basis of their experiences together. Nobody announces it. It just happens. When it does, it changes the whole tenor of the way an organization operates. Leaders without this kind of earned authority have an uphill struggle.

The shift from unearned to earned authority can most easily be illustrated in an audience's reaction to a speaker. As the speaker is introduced with all of his or her credentials, the audience sits politely in judgment. As the speaker launches into the topic, the audience makes up its mind whether the message is relevant and whether the speaker is truly saying important things and merits authority. Unless this shift occurs, the speaker's influence is minimal. An interesting artifact of this transition can be observed in college classes: Students take voluminous notes when unearned authority is high. They take fewer and fewer notes as earned authority takes precedence. You don't have to write down what important people have to say!

Facilitating the Organization

Besides sharing themselves, authentic leaders can contribute in other ways to the formation and functioning of a person-centered organization. For example, a leader can do much to create a climate of warmth and security within a group. The physical environment can be chosen with an eye to comfort, privacy, concentration, and a minimum of interruption to the organization's dialogue, experiments, or interpersonal relationships.

Designated leaders can be keenly aware of the burdens to communication they carry by reason of their job descriptions and "administrivia," and they can seek to defuse such effects by laughing at themselves, acknowledging mistakes or ignorance, expressing enthusiasm for good ideas, and showing appreciation for the sensitivity and contributions of participants. They can contribute to an atmosphere of tolerance and acceptance, avoid judgments and stereotypes, or actively seek to eliminate barriers to participation and communication. Facilitative leaders may even decline a leadership role altogether if that would contribute to the success of the organization's efforts. All these possible ways of behaving are not a matter of acting. Yet they are almost impossible to accomplish effectively unless they are authentic products of the leader's true feelings and beliefs.

Out of Chaos into Order

We have pointed out that organizations are living things. They want to happen. And people are constantly in search of personal fulfillment. They can, will, and must move toward health *if* the way seems open to them to do so. People join groups to increase their chances for fulfillment, and the organizations in which they participate mirror the needs of the members *if* the way seems open for the organization to do so. This may seem like wishful thinking or a doubtful assumption to things-oriented leaders anxious to "get things done."

Allowed to do so, organizations operate in the same way that people grow and students learn. They flounder for awhile, seeking to find out who they are, what they want, and how to achieve those goals. As any teacher knows, the process is sloppy and time consuming. Students begin in confusion or chaos, then bit by bit they find their way to new insights, ideas, and growth. Each learner does this in his or her own individual way. There are strict limits on how much the process can be speeded up or what avenues the search for meaning will follow.

For many leaders or administrators, this concept of organization is maddening. They say, "It takes too much time! What are they doing, going off in those directions? Let's get on with it! We have deadlines to meet!" The whole business of chaos offends their sense of order, control, and direction. The outcome of this, too often, is a breakdown in the process, with everyone losing faith in each other, as in the following example.

> A high school faculty decided that students should be given a lesson in democratic government. They suggested formation of a student council. The students were enthusiastic, and they organized and carried out an election. At the first meeting of the council, students passed a resolution that distressed some faculty members.
>
> The resolution was to have an "open campus," which meant that students could leave campus during lunch or at other times when not in class.
>
> The faculty vetoed the idea, and the students went off to try again. This effort, too, was vetoed by the student council advisor. So were several more. Word quickly got around, and the students gave up on their student government. They treated it like the farce it had become, and the faculty moaned about the students' lack of responsibility. "They treat their own student government as though it was just a game," the faculty declared in outrage. And why not? Who taught the students that their efforts were of little consequence?

It is in the nature of organizations, just as with individuals, to press against their limits. That is how they discover their own strengths and capabilities. If limits must be imposed on organizations, they need to be in place at the start. Organizations can deal with such constraints when they are known from the beginning; limitations imposed after the fact are a different matter. They are likely to be perceived as authoritarian mandates or betrayals of faith, destructive to the very essence of organization.

Of course there are times when limits need to be changed later in a group's operations, as, for example, when a group has drifted from its purpose or a new leader comes into the picture. Limits imposed at such times are a ticklish matter, requiring tact, diplomacy, and straightforward dialogue, probably followed by a period of readjustment in the organization.

Such periods of reorganization also may be observed when personnel of a group changes for whatever reason. Like any other living entity, organizations must spend time and energy adjusting to the removal or addition of parts. Outsiders may see this as a return to chaos, but it is simply a sign of the system's reforming its relationships. Like people, organizations can, will, and must seek fulfillment *if* the way seems open to do so. People participate in groups to find fulfillment for their own needs and personal fulfillment. They leave or give up on groups that do not meet those needs.

Clarity About Expectations and Restraints

Many organizational problems can be eased or resolved by clarifying the objectives of the parties involved. Leaders must be clear about their own objectives, whether they are newcomers to established organizations or establishing new ones. And groups must be clear about the constraints within which they must operate. Without such clarity, all parties are likely to be frustrated.

Earlier, we outlined two basic strategies for working with people: a management strategy and a person-centered one. Each strategy has advantages and disadvantages, different modes of operation, and different goals and expectations. These are not interchangeable, nor can they be switched on and off as occasion seems to demand. It is no easier to switch from the person-centered approach to a management one than it is to move from a democratic society to an autocratic one. All it takes is manipulating the executive's power. For an organization used to a management philosophy, comfort with a person-centered philosophy takes time, experimentation, and freedom to explore and discover the best ways of functioning.

Management is a matter of control and direction; person-centered organizations are processes of growth. Educational leaders can save themselves and those with whom they work much disappointment and frustration by being clear about the strategy in use and governing themselves accordingly.

If the organization is established for a specific purpose and is expected to focus on that matter, those constraints must be clearly communicated to the group, along with the leader's role. If the group is to operate from a person-centered orientation, that also must be clear to all concerned. In the latter case, the organization will arrive at its own role definition and ways of operating. It may need to go through a period of chaos as it sorts out its role and function. It will also need to feel free to make adaptations. That may be difficult for principals or administrators anxious to get the job done or for parents, community members, or others who want to see concrete results. The administrator's own need for order and logic can be sorely pressed, and it may take considerable self-discipline to refrain from interfering in the organization's processes. But once a commitment is made to a person-centered approach, it must be carried through.

Searching for Barriers

Whatever approach to organization an educational leader chooses, modern conceptions of learning and change call for techniques of process facilitation, making it possible for the organization to operate most productively to accomplish its goals. We have seen that human beings do not react efficiently to control and direction.

When dealing with the *people* aspects of leadership, we need to remember that modern conceptions of how people learn and change call for working with people rather than against them, for a facilitating process rather than a controlling one. Much of the educational leader's time and energies must be devoted to easing, supporting, encouraging, and rewarding the processes of organization. One valuable way of doing this is to make a systematic search for the barriers that keep organization members from being involved, then carefully remove them from the path of progress. The process is illustrated in the following anecdote.

> In 1937, Art Combs was a high school teacher in a steel mill town in the Ohio River valley. The city was still in the grip of the Great Depression, and the high school faculty had made a rule that any profit from student events had to be returned to the student body in some fashion.
>
> Combs was advisor of the "Hi Y," and the club was nearing the end of the year. Members were confronted with the problem of how to return the money they had made on several projects back to the student body. At the planning session, various suggestions were raised and rejected. Then, someone suggested a school dance.
>
> "Nah," someone else disagreed. "Lots of kids won't come because they can't dance."
>
> To keep the discussion going, Combs said, "Is there some way we could get everyone to come?"
>
> One ingenious member of the club offered, "The only thing I think might work is if there was some kind of dance that nobody knew how to dance, and we taught them when they got there. That might work."
>
> This started a lively discussion with the conclusion that nobody in the school knew how to square dance. So the club would tell everyone, "Nobody in our school knows how to square dance, so everybody come and we will all learn together." That settled, committees were formed to find a band and caller, decorate the gym, and advertise the affair.
>
> Started on this track, Combs raised the question: "What else would keep people from coming to the dance?" The discussion went like this.

Barrier: "Some guys won't come because they haven't got a date."

Solution: Advertise that this is a stag dance. Nobody can come with a date. Let the boys in one side of the gym and the girls in the other. What happens after that is their business.

Barrier: "Lots of guys and girls won't come because they don't have the right clothes."

Solution: This is a country dance after work. People should come in their everyday clothing.

Barrier: "Guys want to buy their girl something to eat."

Solution: Feed them at the dance. Committees were formed to round up cookies, sodas, and the like from parents and folks in the community.

Barrier: "Nobody has much money, so we need to make it cheap to get in."

Solution: Use the club treasury to subsidize the entrance fee. Make the cost as little as possible without losing money on the affair. With $65 in the club treasury, it was decided to charge 25 cents (which sounds small at today's prices, but not in the Depression).

Club members were excited about the idea, but many scoffed and said it would never work. When the night of the dance arrived, the largest crowd ever filled the gymnasium. Instead of spending its $65, the club still had $35 after expenses!

The lesson learned here was a technique of systematically searching for the barriers to participation and finding ways to negate them. The technique has paid great dividends throughout Combs's career. He has applied it to teaching, administration, counseling, group process, conflict resolution—and even for a year as a lobbyist in the state legislature.

Every group confronts barriers to its functioning. Educational leaders can do much to facilitate group process by a systematic "search and destroy" mission for barriers to participation.

ॐ ॐ ॐ

Authenticity requires that educational leaders be self-revealing, that they be who they are. This facilitates authenticity in those they encounter on or off the job. Consider your own feelings when interacting with authentic or unauthentic people. You usually feel more comfortable and freer to share information—and yourself—with truly authentic people. When dealing with people who are "acting a role" or hiding themselves, you're much more likely to feel uncomfortable, inhibited, and self-defensive.

These same reactions occur in living systems. Organizations operate best when they are free to *be* and *become*. They don't operate as well when they are too constrained or are hampered in fulfilling their tasks. Thus, authentic leaders can contribute to the authenticity and successful operation of organizations by openly sharing themselves and by helping remove barriers from the path of an organization's own reach for authentic fulfillment.

LEADERS AND THEIR ORGANIZATIONS

THE UNITED STATES, LIKE MANY OTHER SOCIETIES, HAS BEEN unbelievably successful in the control and direction of things. We have provided ourselves with food, clothing, shelter, communication, transportation, heating, cooling, light, and energy beyond our ancestors' wildest imaginations, even as recently as 100 years ago. Small wonder, then, that our concepts of leadership are defined in terms of organizational control and direction.

Organizations have long been treated as machines, as ways to get things done. Yet as we have seen in this book, this manipulation-of-forces approach breaks down when applied to people. Organizations of people cannot be successfully controlled and directed like things.

The Traditional View of Organizations

Traditionally, school organizations are established to accomplish a preconceived goal. Members are chosen carefully, each for a specific contribution or task. Once established, school organizations—be they classrooms, teams, committees, departments, or whole schools—

follow orderly rules and regulations. They operate within clearly defined parameters to achieve stipulated objectives. They generally function under the control of a designated leader or supervisor, who is responsible for the organization's direction. Leaders may be "expert" in the task assigned to the organization, or they may be "expert" in management and administration.

Within this frame of reference, organizations are devices to achieve goals in an orderly fashion. We don't doubt that these kinds of organizations have been immensely useful in providing the things of modern society. But it also is clear that this frame of reference breaks down when applied to people.

A New View of Organizations

Only recently have we begun to understand that an organization is not simply a human contrivance but a living, dynamic function of the universe itself. All things exist in some form of organization. From modern physics, biology, systems theory, and chaos theory, we recognize that living things are organizations just like the mountains and prairies of the land, waters of the oceans, or the stars and planets of the universe (Wheatley & Kellner-Rogers, 1996). Organization is in the very nature of things and in people, too.

Organizations of things may be built, managed, or contrived. Organizations of people are another matter. They are living forces that seek to maintain and enhance themselves. Organizations of whatever nature have four characteristics:

1. They tend to maintain and enhance themselves.
2. They are capable of change and adaptation.
3. They have identity or direction.
4. They have force.

People are, themselves, made up of organizations, and they participate in other organizations, ad infinitum. Looking within ourselves, we quickly see that we are composed of organizations within organizations within organizations. We are made up of systems: digestive, reproductive, and immune. The systems, in turn, are composed of tissues, which are composed of cells, which are made up of molecules and atoms. What's more, these organizations constantly affect each other. What happens to smaller organizations affects the larger ones. And what happens to larger organizations affects smaller ones, too.

The same is true for the larger organizations in which each person participates. We participate in clubs, families, relationships, churches, businesses, neighborhoods, cities, states, nations, the world, and the universe itself. All these organizations have identity, stability, fluidity, and strength, and they seek the maintenance and enhancement of their identity and function.

In Chapter 1 we observed that people constantly seek to discover who they are and to maintain and enhance their identity. To facilitate that process they join organizations that seem likely to contribute to their self-fulfillment. People remain loyal to organizations that contribute to that end. When groups no longer fill their needs, people try to change the organization or leave to find some more satisfying one.

Reconceiving organizations as living, dynamic events demands widespread changes in thinking about the nature and functions of school organizations and about educational leadership. Organizations of people must be treated as growing, creative events—not machines. If they are allowed to, organizations will seek fulfillment, to be and become, just like each member.

Organizations cannot be understood as the mere sum of their parts. They have the capacity to grow from within as a consequence of the interactions of their participants. Though they may begin in chaos, they seek an identity and reach for its enhancement. That is the nature of growth, and it proceeds automatically—*if* it is free to do so. This is what our forefathers in the United States knew when they designed the nation on the principle that, "When people are free, they can find their own best ways."

Organizations can do what their members alone could not. Even more important, they have the capacity to transcend limitations in creative ways some might consider impossible given the nature of their membership. Perhaps the best example of this power is seen in legislative assemblies. These bodies are cross-sections of the general public. They are made up of average citizens with a few brilliant minds and a few not so brilliant minds among them, just like the rest of the population. Nevertheless, year after year, they manage to govern successfully, producing legislation in the public interest. Of course, we may doubt this in the heat of political campaigns or when legislatures take actions contrary to cherished personal beliefs. In the long run, however, legislatures do remarkably well. The genius of democracy lies in the fact that together people can, indeed, find their own best ways.

Effective organizations grow from within like all other living things. They fulfill their identity in supportive conditions, but they are stunted or distorted by mismanagement and control. Whether organizations grow and prosper or wither and die depends on the leader's belief systems. School organizations, too, share these universal characteristics of organizations.

Nurturing a thriving organization is like growing a healthy plant: You get the best seeds possible and plant them in the best ground available. Then you surround them with the best conditions for growth, such as water, sunlight, and nutrients. Then you get out of the way and let the plants grow. You don't arbitrarily weed out healthy seedlings, withhold light and water, or demand that the plants be radishes when you actually planted sunflower seeds. You do not shout, "Grow! Damn you! Grow!" Living systems do not respond well to this kind of coercion and direction, and neither do organizations.

How Organizations Grow

Organizations normally start out in chaos, seeking identity as members interact with one another. They start, stop, back up, turn around, jump forward, raise questions, propose actions, ask, and argue. Little by little, if they are successful, they create an identity. Members discover each other's capacities and contributions, and the organization takes on a structure and function focused toward its fulfillment.

An organization is a living, dynamic entity, and just by listening to the level of dialogue, it is possible to assess the level of personal involvement and commitment. This often is illustrated through the level of talk as a group develops its unique structure and function.

In the beginning, conversation generally occurs at "fingertip length," like interactions at a reception or cocktail party. People discuss safe topics like football or the latest movies, conversation that requires little personal involvement. They speak in descriptive terms:

- I saw . . .
- Did you hear . . . ?
- Did you read where . . . ?
- My uncle once . . .

As people get to know each other better, talk becomes more personal, but it still has a built-in escape:

- I read that . . .
- Once I . . .
- What do you think about . . . ?
- I once knew somebody who . . .

As people feel safer, conversation begins to include the self, at first very tentatively:

- I sometimes think that . . .
- I'm not sure I agree with . . .
- I wonder if . . . ?
- I thought, maybe . . .

As the group becomes closer, people are more straightforward. They make statements like these:

- I believe that . . .
- I read that . . . but I don't believe . . .
- It seems to me that . . .
- I believe . . . and here's why: . . .

As people get closer still, you begin to hear their feelings and emotions:

- I felt bad about . . .
- I'm pretty doubtful about . . .
- I like, dislike, worry about, wish that . . .

When participants feel truly safe and involved, they begin to talk about feelings with passion:

- It makes me so angry when . . !
- I feel happy, sad, anxious, sympathy for . . .

And when folks are *really* into it, they say things like: I love, hate, want to, am moved, am overcome!

The process of developing an identity and fulfilling a function takes time. Organizations, like people, begin from vague possibilities. They develop a sense of self or identity and start to discover what they can do and cannot do. They also develop a sense of purpose or a goal, and they explore techniques for getting there. We can see this happen in the growth of a human being. It happens in organizations, as well—*if* they are free to do so.

Unfortunately, a things-oriented, manipulation-of-forces culture insists on treating most organizations as machines, as structures designed to produce some prescribed outcome. This kind of culture cannot wait for an organization to find its identity, discover its purposes, define its strengths and limitations, or choose its own methods to achieve its goals. Instead of working with the processes of growth, a manipulation-of-forces approach seeks to make things happen. It does not nurture the system and get out of its way to let it do its thing. It hampers organizations with inadequate funds, equipment, or information; demands to meet deadlines; and requirements to work in designated ways to produce a designated product.

Of course, educational leaders do not interfere with organizational functioning because they are vicious and spiteful. The realities of their jobs often require a management approach. For example, parents, the community, school boards, legislatures, or college admission standards may mandate goals. Leaders may have to limit organizations because of time constraints or budget considerations. Many of these factors are inherent in the educational system and have hindered reform for generations. They also make it necessary to recognize the importance of the two kinds of organizational patterns: a management approach and a person-centered one.

We need both types of approaches in education. Tackling problems with two tools is almost always better than using only one. Person-centered thinking about organizations offers a second way of designing and facilitating school organizations. The problem for educational leaders is to understand management and person-centered approaches well enough to know when each will best advance educational processes and facilitate their optimum functions.

To make this choice effectively, educational leaders need to recognize that traditional educational leadership in a things-oriented, manipulation-of-forces culture is almost exclusively preoccupied with the management approach. Powerful forces indoctrinate educational leaders in the exclusive use of the manipulation-of-forces concept. These forces also ignore the fact that dealing with people and groups calls for a person-centered frame of reference. However, ignoring the living qualities of organizations comes at a price.

The Methods of Educational Leadership

When leaders understand that organizations are living, dynamic agencies, they reconceive leadership in a new perspective. They can be leaders (managers, controllers, directors) when dealing with things. But dealing with human beings calls for facilitators: helpers, aides, assistors, ministers to a process. This requires educational leaders to wear two hats, as managers and facilitators. They also must know when each role is appropriate.

Whatever their role, educators constantly seek "right" methods for dealing with problems. When they confront a problem, most teachers or administrators first ask, "How can I? What should I do?" These questions are holdovers from the manipulation-of-forces concept of working with things.

Every educator needs a trustworthy assortment of appropriate methods. The assumption, however, that there are right or universal methods is a fallacy. There can be no universal, "right" methods in human relationships. A review of hundreds of research studies designed to find trustworthy, "right" methods illustrates the conclusion that there simply are no right or universal methods for any role in education (Elena, Stevenson, & Webb, 1961). There are good reasons for this conclusion.

In the first place, methods are not simple. In fact, they are highly complex. For example, the methods teachers use must fit the conditions: the room temperature, lighting, furnishings, equipment, materials, and more. They also must fit the curriculum: where students are, what has gone before, teachers' goals, and the school's philosophy and goals. Methods also must fit the students in all their complexity, needs, intelligence, health, interests, and emotional condition. Add to all those variables the complexity of the teacher's needs, goals, knowledge, belief system, feelings, and aspirations, and it becomes clear why there can never be a "right" method of teaching or leading.

The crucial fact about methods is that they must fit the time and place when someone is taking action. Even then they may not be appropriate an instant later. If methods are to fit, they must be unique. By definition, there can be no such thing as a common uniqueness (Combs, 1992).

Even if we could discover some promising method, we still could not rely on it. The effect of any method is not inherent in the method itself. The effect will be determined by what the recipient of the method thinks is happening. The search for universal right methods is thus an exercise in futility.

Two General Strategies for Organizations

Although we cannot hope to find universal right methods, it is possible to design some general strategies. Drawing on person-centered findings about people and how they learn and change, we can describe two general approaches: managerial and person-centered. Each approach represents a frame of reference for handling problems of learning and change, and each has critical implications for educational leadership.

The management approach to organization follows the behavioral objectives model of industry. It begins with a clearly defined objective, selects the techniques needed to reach it, puts the plan into action, then assesses the outcome to determine if the objective was achieved. That approach to organization has been very useful, and it is the way people have dealt with things for hundreds of years. It also has widespread appeal to school boards, traditional teachers and administrators, parents, and legislators. They are used to this way of thinking. It seems so straightforward, logical, and businesslike that few people even stop to question it. It has been the preferred approach for dealing with education for many generations.

The person-centered strategy for organizations, on the other hand, follows a growth model. It often operates without clear-cut objectives. One convenes a group to confront a problem, then searches for solutions whose nature cannot be clearly discerned in the beginning. This is the strategy that counselors use in helping a client explore personal problems. It is also the strategy used by a legislature debating an issue, by a scientist seeking a cure for cancer, or by a teacher using modern "discovery" methods. Unfortunately, person-centered approaches are far less understood in our society and consequently much less used.

To contrast the two approaches, imagine how they might be applied to the problem of improving the lives of people in inner cities.

> Operating from the managerial strategy, a social work administrator sitting in his office devised an exciting plan. Why not have the city's service clubs "Adopt a Block" in the inner city and provide the means to upgrade the neighborhood? Broaching the plan to several service clubs, he was delighted to get their assent. With their commitments in hand, he met with people on various blocks and enthusiastically set forth the proposal. He was totally unprepared for their reaction. The people felt demeaned and insulted by the proposition. They angrily told the social worker, "Forget your plan! We don't need your help!"
>
> Some years later, another social worker, operating from a person-centered approach, had more success. She joined the neighborhood groups. After some months, a member of one of the groups suggested, "Why don't we get some of the rich folks in our city to help with our neighborhood projects?" People were intrigued with the idea, and, after much debate, the plan was adopted. Instead of "Adopt a Block," however, they called their plan, "Block Power!" A majority of the community got into the act. A committee was formed to select appropriate projects, and another laid its proposals before the city's service clubs. The clubs approved the projects. Shortly after, the projects were underway.

Whichever strategy for educational leadership is chosen, it inevitably commits the organization to a whole series of consequences. Figure 9.1 contrasts these in chart form. In the figure, the "closed system" corresponds in many ways to the management strategy; the "open system," to the person-centered approach.

Because most educational leaders are already familiar with the management strategy for organizations, the rest of this chapter considers person-centered concepts and organizations as living systems.

Figure 9.1. Open and Closed Systems of Thinking in Reform

Topic	Closed System	Open System
The focus	• Behavior management, control, or manipulation • Based on behavioristic psychology	• Process oriented— facilitating conditions • Based on perceptual- experiential psychology
The leader	• Expert diagnostician • Total responsibility • Precise goals or skills • Director, manipulator of forces and outcome	• Guide, helper • Responsibility shared • Broader goals • Consultant, aide, facilitator
Curriculum	• Oughts and shoulds • Right answers • Prepare for world • Specific goals, grades, and evaluation	• Process goals • Creation of conditions • Problem centered • Fill needs, create new ones
Techniques	• Industrial model • Competition and evaluation valued • Administration dominant • Emphasis on goal achievement	• Personal growth model • Cooperative effort; problem centered • Many group decisions • Emphasis on intelligent problem solving
Philosophy	• Control and direction • "Great leader" concept • Doubts about motivation	• Growth philosophy • Democratic • Trust in human organism
Participants	• Passive • Leader seen as enemy • Dependent • Lack commitment • Conformity valued • Endurance of stress	• Active, responsible • Leader seen as helper • Participate in decisions • Involved • Creativity valued • Concern for others
Values	• Simple skills • Ends clearly known • Conditions for change clearly in leader's hands	• Broad goals • Ends not precisely predictable • Humane concerns prominent

Source: Adapted by permission from *The Schools We Need: New Assumptions for Educational Reform* (p. 71), by A. W. Combs, 1991, New York: University Press.

Organizations as Living Systems

The goals or mandates for person-centered organizations are generally broad, even vague. Most organizations of this type operate to address problems or questions. They also may be established with open-ended goals like, "Let's get together to talk about what it means to be a man (or woman) in the '90s" or "What is it we are really trying to do in this school?" Or groups simply may get together: to dance, listen to music, or hang out and see what happens.

This is the way individual people learn and grow. It is also the way in which living systems operate, a process of search and discovery. A things-oriented, manipulation-of-forces society does not prepare us to work in this fashion. Accordingly, observing living organizations in operation may be distressing for people who are anxious to get things done. People who join person-centered groups and are unused to working in this fashion may take some time to learn how.

Expected Chaos

It is normal for living organizations to begin in apparent chaos. Chaos, however, is anathema to the need for order and predictability demanded by traditional cultures, logic, the "scientific method," and traditional concepts of administration. It also is unacceptable to leaders who seek to maintain a static system or bureaucracy. Modern theorists and practitioners now recognize that chaos is not the complete breakdown of order we have formerly supposed. Rather, it is an orderly phenomenon in which a newly forming organization or a disrupted one finds a new way of being. Chaos is thus a step in becoming something new, different, or more fulfilling. The seeming confusion of a living organization as it explores and defines itself, then, must be seen as a normal process of growth.

Anyone who has watched the explorations of adolescents as they seek to define their identities is familiar with such chaos. They also can attest to the feelings of frustration this causes for observers of the process. What seems like chaos in living systems is actually part of a process. To lose patience or interfere can delay or kill off the organization's search and discovery for its identity, mission, and achievements.

Change and Threat

Living organizations work best in an atmosphere that is challenging but not threatening. Chapter 2 described the negative effects of threat. It produces tunnel vision and self-defense, neither of which are conducive to participation. Leaders working toward person-centered organizations need, therefore, to give careful attention to creating an atmosphere with the fewest possible barriers to individual involvement. Among the factors to consider are the comfort and equipment of the workplace; an adjustable time frame; and, of course, the leader's skill. Ideally, living systems operate best in an atmosphere of friendly cooperation where personal involvement is encouraged and facilitated.

The manipulation-of-forces approach to dealing with problems is so native to the U.S. culture that few people have had the opportunity to experience truly person-centered organizations. As a consequence, people generally must learn new ways of working with one another. For example, effective person-centered organizations require their participants to be skilled with active listening. That is, coworkers need the capacity to truly listen to what other people are trying to express. This is a rare quality in most of the interchanges in U.S. culture.

To get some idea of how infrequent this kind of personal attention is, try requiring the participants in a conversation to first accurately repeat the gist of the previous speaker's remarks before the next person can talk. This is only one of the adjustments participants have to confront as a person-centered group finds itself, settles on an agenda, and develops a drive toward fulfillment. Participants must also experiment with various levels of participation, decide how far they can trust each other, and resolve how willing they are to fully engage in the process. An outsider watching all this go on sees an organization in chaos and may not recognize that this is all a part of the process.

Many school leaders are ill equipped to work in person-centered organizations. They have never encountered such groups in the course of their training, and they have been so deeply involved with the "things" aspects of their jobs that they have had little or no opportunity to study the living organizations in which they work, much less reflect on their operations. Because person-centered organizations are not generally understood by people who have never experienced them, they may be unappreciated and harshly criticized. When that happens, educational leaders can be of real help by protecting organizations until they reach a point where their outcomes can be observed and properly evaluated. Even if they lack the skills to lead person-centered organizations, school leaders can recognize their value and facilitate their functions.

A major problem in current educational reform is the attempt to solve all problems by manipulating forces. Consequently, many problems are addressed by some new method or technique with little or no consideration for basic assumptions about the problem. Leaders forever seek to plug leaks in the system, but they rarely look at underlying causes. This results in techniques or methods that are introduced as surefire solutions, but they soon turn out to be just another stop-gap effort.

Few human problems are solved by simple manipulation of external forces. The causes of human behavior lie inside people and are only partly affected by external events. Effective solutions, therefore, must generally come about through changes in human beliefs, attitudes, feelings, hopes, or aspirations. Trying to change what goes on in a classroom, for example, is seldom accomplished by fiat from the front office. Real change comes about as teachers modify their beliefs. When that happens, they change their behavior without external stimuli.

A major value of living organizations is that they provide opportunities for participants to engage in dialogue, explore, experiment, and evaluate ideas and behaviors. They are breeding places for ideas and innovation, two elements desperately needed as schools head into the 21st century. Innovation is a product of creativity, which in turn is stimulated by dialogue and human interaction. Conformity and creativity do not go well together. If we ask people to conform, they are unlikely to be very creative. On the other hand, if we want folks to be creative, it is practically certain they will have problems with demands to conform. Management organizations often ensure, or even improve on, the status quo; only rarely do they result in truly creative innovations.

Choosing an Organizational Strategy

In this chapter we have drawn sharp contrasts between management and person-centered organizations and their implications for practice. This contrast is intentional, to distinguish between the two positions. Such sharp contrasts do not ordinarily appear in daily practice. As we pointed out earlier, the management approach works in some contexts, thus contributing to "partly right" methods. Those individuals whose belief systems support a person-centered approach, however, can handle daily management tasks while using empathy, showing authenticity, and demonstrating trust in the human organism.

Generally speaking, management organizations can be useful in situations where outcomes are clearly and simply defined in advance and when the means to control events are firmly in the leader's grasp. The strategy is particularly useful when dealing with things. Effectiveness rapidly disintegrates, however, as the need to cope with people and their interactions with each other becomes more critical. Person-centered thinking generally proves more useful when there are broad goals; when specific objectives cannot be spelled out in finite terms; and when dealing with matters requiring change in people's inner experiences, feelings, attitudes, beliefs, values, and personal meanings.

Next to the family, education is the most people-intensive institution in most cultures. In the United States, it is the institution we have invented to induct youth into our culture and to facilitate the personal and societal growth of citizens. One would expect, then, that it essentially would be people-oriented, but educational critics frequently complain that schools are more expressive of a things-oriented, manipulation-of-forces way of being. Educational institutions more often model control and direction than facilitation of learning and growth. Seeing schools as living organisms may help to resolve that paradox.

The concept of organizations as living organisms applies to groups of whatever kind and description: classrooms, clubs, teams, committees, even whole schools or educational systems. These groups can be facilitated or inhibited in the same fashion as any other living thing. Thinking of organizations as living systems is a new approach for educators, and we have only begun to think about its implications. Who knows where it will take us? These ideas seem to have potential for vastly changing the education system as we know it today even if the concept still needs much exploration.

Participation in person-centered organizations makes important contributions to the learning process itself. People learn all sorts of things from their experiences in organizations, often more significantly and permanently than the intended purpose for which the organization was formed. Learning to cooperate and work for the common good, for example, is an important value for healthy personal growth, as well as a vital lesson for future citizens. So, also, are feelings of identification, respect for diversity, and being involved in "something much bigger than myself." Healthy human beings are characterized by positive views of self, acceptance of reality, and deep feelings of oneness with others. All these are acquired from experience in interpersonal relationships. They are also human qualities necessary for successful living and working in a democratic society.

Working with and participating in person-centered organizations is valuable for educational leaders, too. Living organizations make important contributions to an educator's personal and professional growth. The achievements of educational organizations obviously contribute to the success and prestige of administrators, principals, supervisors, and superintendents. But leaders willing and able to work successfully with and in living systems also discover how the experience can ease, even solve, knotty problems of interrelationships with staff and colleagues. The sense of community that living systems engender can go far to reduce the stresses of a leader's responsibility and ease the loneliness of administration. Communication may be improved, roles can be clarified and accepted, and mutual admiration and respect can thrive. Though the concept of the school as a living system is new to education, it obviously holds out the promise of some valuable benefits.

The Person-Centered Preparation of School Leaders

FOR YEARS, EDUCATIONAL LEADERSHIP PREPARATION programs have concentrated on teaching specific leadership traits and the "right" methods for managing organizations. They have taught prospective administrators how to develop budgets, schedules, and curriculum; how to control and supervise people; how to manage time effectively; and how to apply legal precedents to the everyday world of schools. Even today, the content and pedagogy of most administration courses specifically are designed to teach graduate students to focus on things, not people. Throughout this book, however, we have emphasized the importance of human relationships and the necessity for focusing on people, not things. An emphasis on human beings, or a person-centered view, suggests that people do not respond directly to forces exerted on them; rather, they behave according to the meanings that exist for them at a given time.

We also have emphasized that effective leadership is composed of more than knowledge about specific subject matter or "right" methods. Effective leadership is a function of a leader's beliefs. Effective leaders view themselves and others in positive ways. They approach their tasks from an internal frame of reference and are attuned to how things seem to the people with whom they work. They seek to realize positive, socially constructive, and personally fulfilling purposes.

This chapter explores implications of the person-centered view for leadership preparation programs. We suggest that these programs should focus on different assumptions and develop new curriculums and instructional strategies. We also make the case that preparation programs must focus on helping school leaders develop their interpersonal relationship skills. We envision programs where prospective school leaders immerse themselves in real-life issues; engage in authentic dialogue to make meaning from their experiences; and participate in group processes, role playing, and simulation activities.

These kinds of learning experiences will prepare future school leaders for developing person-centered schools. But for universities to actively promote the kind of leadership we espouse, they too will have to undergo massive changes. Just as school reform and restructuring generated role changes for principals and teachers, so, too, higher education must change.

Reexamining Higher Education

If they are to make a difference in developing effective school leaders, universities first must reexamine their cultures. As Roberts observed in 1990, "To cultivate and develop school leaders who can meet the challenges of new structures and reforming school practices will require a dismantling and restructuring of the ways in which such leaders are prepared and trained" (p. 135).

At most institutions of higher education, the culture is fraught with elitism, competition, and isolation. Unfortunately, the existing reward structure honors faculty members' research and publication records. Although teaching and service are lauded as critical aspects of faculty performance, the reality is that most universities reward faculty members who focus on research.

Because they are rewarded for empirical research, these faculty members have few incentives to engage in meaningful dialogue and partnerships with K–12 educators (Barnett & Whitaker, 1996). Thus, they seldom spend time in public schools—and practitioners rarely read their publications. The United States has a history where the K–12 and university levels remain distinctly separate. But greater linkages between K–12 schools and institutions of higher education will be necessary to better prepare future school leaders.

Linking K–12 and Higher Education

Many groups have called for stronger links between K–12 and higher education, in particular for teacher and administrator preparation programs (see, for example, Holmes Group, 1986; National Commission on Excellence in Education Administration, 1987). For this to happen, professors and deans must be willing to become partners with teachers and administrators in the K–12 setting. The two systems need more information exchange and more authentic communication. Moreover, the traditional hierarchy that exists between the two systems, with higher education at the top, must be dismantled.

A good example of this hierarchy is how higher education controls the K–12 curriculum. Schools are so worried that their standards will not mesh with what higher education desires that they change the curriculum according to what universities want. In many cases, these changes are inappropriate for K–12 schools. Perhaps universities should change *their* curriculums rather than prescribe standards for K–12 education.

In essence, new attitudes, norms, and practices are desperately needed. Some stronger links between K–12 schools and universities have emerged in recent years. These links often occur in the form of partnerships where universities develop ongoing relationships with selected school sites. Professional development schools, or partner schools, offer a place for prospective leaders to practice what they have experienced in preparation programs and to engage in inquiry about real-life problems. Graduate students resolve challenges alongside teachers and principals. Partner schools also offer graduate students places to conduct field experiences, practicums, and internships. Through these kinds of experiences, students work in varied school sites for larger blocks of time under the guidance of mentors who are actual school leaders.

Students who spend significant amounts of time in schools early in preparation programs connect their readings and coursework to real-life issues. Bridging university training with fieldwork allows students to reflect on and make meaning of the work. Principals and university professors also benefit when theory, research, and daily practice are connected through mutual reflection.

Escaping the isolation that plagues practicing administrators and professors requires creativity. Many professors have not worked in schools for a number of years, and many lack any administrative experience. By the same token, the world of the professorship is foreign to most administrators. How often do principals say, "Those professors are so closed up in their ivory towers that they haven't a clue what the real world of schools is like!" In a similar vein, university professors complain, "I wish those teachers and principals really understood the value of research and theory. If they would just pay attention to research, their schools would be much better places!" These kinds of comments illustrate the lack of conversation and understanding between the two groups.

One way to avoid this unhappy picture is to support processes and structures that enable practitioners and professors to trade places for a period of time. Both public schools and universities can establish job-sharing programs, coupled with incentives, that encourage such linkages. For example, why not invite a professor of educational administration to trade places with a principal or assistant principal for a semester, or even a year? Or, make arrangements for teacher education professors to job-share with K–12 classroom teachers. What a difference these arrangements would make in both worlds!

Changing Curriculum and Instruction

Professors of educational administration have long debated the issue of appropriate content for their programs and courses. The debate continues as the roles of school leaders evolve. No one questions the fact that school leaders need to be well-informed. But well-informed about what? Several factors make it difficult to determine exactly what school leaders need to know.

For example, thanks to technology, many people have access to more information than they could ever want or need. Television, CD-ROMs, and the Internet all have fueled an information explosion. How can leadership preparation programs include all the information a person needs to function as a principal? They can't.

It is impossible to define a curriculum that must be required of everyone. The world is more complex and complicated than it was even two or three decades ago. Because of societal changes, we expect schools today to assume the responsibilities of parent, social service agency, and health provider, to name a few. These responsibilities require that principals develop many different kinds of skills, but they especially need skills for working with people.

In short, no program can provide a school leader with the "right" information for today's world. What a principal needs to know will depend on the context in which he or she works. It will be determined by the school level and age of children, community context, diversity within the school community, the socioeconomic level of children's families, the extent of school resources, and students' backgrounds and needs, to name only a few factors. One commonality is that we need school leaders who can think and problem solve, express empathy, and embody a strong moral and ethical character.

A major problem in leadership preparation programs is professors' beliefs that if they provide an abundance of content, behavior automatically will change. A story about a man and his dog illustrates the error in this belief.

> A fellow passed his neighbor one day. The man was excited to share the news that he had taught his dog how to talk.
>
> The neighbor said, "That is amazing! Would you ask the dog to say a few words?"
>
> The dog's owner replied, "Oh, I taught him, but he can't actually talk."

This story seems silly at first, until we think about the similarities to what often happens in higher education. A great deal of teaching occurs, but does it change behavior? Professors seem to believe that they need to cover vast amounts of material at a frenzied pace, which reduces the time necessary for discovering meaning. Yet a basic principle in perceptual psychology is as follows: "Any item of information will affect an individual's behavior only in the degree to which he or she has discovered its personal meaning for him/her" (Combs, 1974, p. 33).

Creating Person-Centered Programs

Person-centered learning experiences require a balanced focus on cultivating human relationships, building capacity for all individuals, and developing human potential. Such learning experiences yield authentic dialogue among participants; concentrated inquiry about belief systems; and the challenge of examining assumptions about teaching, learning, and leadership. Rather than adding more and more program requirements to ensure that future administrators have enough information about developing budgets and schedules, the "curriculum in reconstructed preparation programs should be characterized by authenticity, complexity, and interrelatedness" (Murphy, 1992, p. 147).

In addition, the learning experiences in preparation programs should be *real*. Fortunately, a few programs are experimenting with problem-based learning, where prospective leaders collaborate with practitioners, professors, and colleagues to solve real school problems (Bridges, 1992). Through this type of learning experience, students encounter authentic problems of practice. They are immersed in depth rather than breadth, and they receive guidance in how to critically analyze important matters facing a school. Moreover, prospective leaders practice reflection and critical inquiry, and they come to realize the complexity and interrelatedness of problems in schools today.

In problem-based learning, students work in project teams with a faculty member who serves as a resource. Students or instructors present a problem, and students identify learning issues they wish to explore (Bridges, 1992). In problem-based learning, schools often arrange for a professor to bring in a group of graduate students who are willing to work on an issue with the principal and staff. A project team might consist of five to seven graduate students. Each student assumes a primary role, such as project leader, facilitator, recorder, or team member. Depending on the duration of the project, roles might change over time.

For example, one elementary school principal contacted a professor for assistance in expanding parent involvement. The professor recruited six graduate students who were willing to work with the school during the semester. The graduate students surveyed parents, staff, and students; met with parent and community groups; and developed a plan for the school to try the following year. The graduate students learned about the issues surrounding parent involvement from a principal's perspective, and the school community was delighted to have the graduate students' expertise and a plan for the next year.

Using problem-based learning in leadership preparation programs meets three basic conditions for effective learning. First, students select projects they're interested in and want to know more about. This creates a "need to know" critical to their learning. Second, problem-based learning fosters an atmosphere where exploration of personal meaning is possible. With appropriate facilitation by the professor, graduate students explore the meaning the project holds for them personally. Third, the professor can help members of the project group explore their personal meanings together, facilitating the group's dialogue about what was gained from the experience. Although the professor can help, encourage, and assist, it is important that the project group have a sense of self-direction and a sense of responsibility. It would be wrong for a professor to interfere with and direct the work of the project team. Team members must feel they are responsible for their work, and the professor working with the team must value its self-direction.

We believe that most participants in leadership preparation programs have few opportunities to critically analyze real problems or to examine their own belief systems and challenge their assumptions about teaching and learning. These opportunities must be present throughout a leadership preparation program. How else will future administrators learn how to make critical decisions, develop a strong philosophical base from which to operate, or tackle ethical dilemmas that arise so frequently in the daily work of administration?

Changing Instruction

Simply referring to the terms "instruction" and "delivery systems" as we have for years connotes images of bureaucratic structures, delivery of information, and a general feeling of coldness. If we expect school leaders to assume the new roles we have discussed, what better place to learn and practice these roles than in preparation programs?

Meaningful learning experiences depend largely on the instructor's effectiveness. One of the most important aspects of effective teaching, regardless of level, is how the teacher views other people. Research indicates that effective and ineffective teaching can be distinguished with respect to how the teacher views people (Combs, 1974). Again, these beliefs are just as important in higher education as in K–12. The following beliefs about people have enormous implications for how faculty members interact with adult learners.

- **Able/Unable.** The effective professor perceives others as having the capacities to deal with problems and successfully find adequate solutions.
- **Friendly/Unfriendly.** Effective professors see others as being friendly and enhancing. They view others as well-intentioned, not poor-intentioned.
- **Worthy/Unworthy.** The effective professor sees others as worthy and possessing dignity and integrity. The professor does not view them as worthless and unimportant.
- **Internally/Externally Motivated.** The effective professor sees people and their behavior as developing from within rather than as a product of external events. He or she sees people as creative and dynamic, not passive or inert.
- **Dependable/Undependable.** The effective professor sees people as trustworthy and dependable. He or she regards their behavior as understandable, not capricious, unpredictable, or negative.
- **Helpful/Hindering.** The effective professor sees people as being fulfilling and enhancing to self rather than threatening. He or she regards people as important sources of satisfaction rather than sources of frustration and suspicion.

Unfortunately, many preparation programs downplay the importance of adults genuinely interacting and sharing with one another. They also restrict them from forming authentic relationships with faculty members and other practicing administrators. They do not rely on what we know about adult learning: that it should be personalized, active, and collaborative. Instead, much of the learning is professor directed, using a lecture format to present facts. Used exclusively, the lecture method reinforces passive learning, regurgitation of isolated facts, thoughtlessness, and impersonal relationships.

No matter how well content is presented, it will have little effect on students until they become personally involved in the learning process. Learning is not passive. It is active and engaging, and it requires a good deal of personal commitment by the learner. Many professors still use strategies that violate these principles.

There are many ways to ensure that students' learning is active rather than passive. Removing various threats in the learning environment is probably the best way to encourage active participation. Humiliating remarks, put-downs, and rejections are threatening behaviors used too frequently in higher education. Such kinds of behavior cause students to close down to learning experiences, and they create a "turtle in the shell" phenomenon. A turtle is not likely to venture out of its shell unless it feels safe to do so. So it is with human beings when they perceive threat. People learn and grow best if they are not constantly afraid of making mistakes.

Competition for grades is an additional threat in many preparation programs. Grades limit and inhibit learning because students are more concerned about what the professor wants to read or hear rather than immersing themselves deeply in the learning experience. The kind of knowing required for getting an A leaves little room for a student's own purposes or involvement (Combs, 1974). Students quickly learn what the professor wants; they don't focus on their own needs and understanding. Unfortunately, the professor often wants students to know an abundance of details that have little meaning in their everyday lives. For example, professors want students to know how to do a school budget. Why should a significant amount of classroom time be devoted to budgets when this skill can best be learned during a field experience?

Leadership preparation programs need an atmosphere of challenge, discovery, freedom from threat, and personalization. Excellent professors focus more on furthering *processes* than on achieving goals. Processes must be used to enable self-discovery and individual growth. These processes include helping rather than dominating, understanding rather than condemning, demonstrating sensitivity rather than insensitivity, and valuing integrity rather than violating integrity. Extensive dialogue between the instructor and participants, as well as among the participants themselves, also facilitates learning and self-discovery.

Dialogue and open communication pave the way for deeper understanding and personal meaning to emerge. Competent university professors model the skills of facilitation and authentic listening. They accept the responsibility to be available to students and acknowledge interpersonal involvement and relationships as top priorities. They honor the principles of adult learning by recognizing the unique characteristics of individual students, and they also value students' prior experiences.

Effective learning processes also involve group learning activities that demonstrate the importance of teamwork, collaboration, and collegiality. Rather than lecturing for two or three hours, professors would better serve student needs if they devised simulation activities, case studies, or role-playing activities to enhance dialogue, engagement, personal meaning, and relevance. It is only through these kinds of activities that students can learn the group-process skills of listening and communication. Authentic listening and communication skills are learned only through practice and receiving feedback from others. Effective group activities call for an instructor who is not necessarily a content expert but is skilled in assisting the processes of learning and discovering meaning. These activities also call for an instructor who is adept at understanding human nature and interpersonal relationships.

The quality of the learning experience also will be affected by the extent to which students make important decisions affecting their learning. How often have you seen graduate classes where the instructor lays out every detail regarding course objectives, materials, instructional strategies, and assessments? Graduate students who are preparing to be school leaders often have more experiences from which to draw than the professors! So it makes much more sense for these adults to make significant decisions regarding their learning.

Personalizing Learning with Cohort Groups

Cohort groups are one means to actively practice the skills of fostering collaboration and building relationships. In this arrangement, students learn with one another over several months or even years. Groups of students move through their preparation program together, a structure that "promotes the development of community, contributes to enhanced academic rigor, and personalizes an otherwise anonymous set of experiences for students" (Murphy, 1993, p. 239).

The benefits of using cohort groups are similar to programs where teachers work with the same group of students for several years. It is critical for school leaders to be able to form authentic relationships and personalize their learning experiences. Cohort groups strengthen these skills. Other benefits include the availability of all faculty in a program rather than one faculty member per course. In a cohort experience, groups of students work with teachers, parents, and principals on real problems in a school. These experiences enhance problem-centered learning, collaboration, and relevance between university learning experiences and school issues.

All learning experiences in leadership preparation programs should emphasize reflection. Professors must include opportunities for students to critically examine and reflect on past and present experiences as they relate to their roles as educational leaders. Students should be encouraged to share their experiences as integral parts of classroom activities. This kind of reflection might be accomplished through reflective writing exercises that are shared with colleagues, personal journals, or revisiting and sharing educational platforms at various intervals throughout the program. It is through reflection that students enhance the meaning they have derived from learning experiences.

Envisioning New Learning Experiences

A few leadership preparation programs are beginning to reconceptualize learning experiences to recognize new leadership roles. When developing new learning experiences, some essential questions include: What content and field experiences are important sources of knowledge, skills, and attitudes for school leaders? How do these kinds of understanding contribute to the formation of individual beliefs? There are no "right" methods and no "right" curriculum for leadership preparation, but the following sections depict several possible learning experiences that will focus learners' efforts on person-centered thinking.

Developing a Personal Belief System

The content of this learning experience (Barnett et al., 1992) would include an examination of belief systems, the development of an educational platform, team-building exercises, and inquiry about current assumptions that drive leadership and schooling. The importance of self-concept, openness to experience, and developing a sense of identification are examined. Within this learning experience, adults articulate their beliefs, challenge one another in a comfortable surrounding, and experience individual and group success. These experiences encourage participants to develop belief systems that are comprehensive, internally consistent, and personally relevant. Although it may be painful to some to "know thyself," it is imperative that aspiring leaders engage in this process.

Developing the Self in Others

This learning experience would include activities that deal with conflict resolution and mediation, adult learning and development, team building, and staff evaluation and professional growth. Emphasis is placed on developing the self-concepts of others and addressing conflict among teachers, students, parents, and community members. Several important principles of adult learning and development are integrated into this learning experience, such as the importance of accumulated life experiences, adult development issues, and the sociocultural context within which learners work and live. In addition, new learning experiences would include an understanding of perceptual psychology (such as group process skills), a recognition of the importance of empathy, and an understanding of the role of an objective third party trying to resolve conflict between two individuals or groups.

Understanding External Environments

In this experience, students are exposed to issues related to multiculturalism, diversity, multiple realities of experience, working with political agencies, developing links with the community, and how educators work with the external environment. They also might examine the leaders' roles in helping parents and community members be more informed partners in the decision-making process and working collaboratively with school boards.

Interpreting Dynamic Organizations

This learning experience helps adults understand the differences between person-centered and management-centered organizations, the fluidity and complexity within organizations, how organizations grow and change, and the leader's responsibility in dynamic organizations. Emphasis is placed on developing new ways to view organizations, organizational chaos, and developing and comprehending organizational culture.

Examining Moral and Ethical Leadership

Because the development of moral purpose is so crucial for educational leaders, a learning experience is devoted to examining different ethical frameworks and examining the moral and ethical dilemmas school leaders face. Students consider how people have different assumptions and experiences that affect the manner in which they view problems. Emphasis is placed on understanding individual belief systems and how these belief systems affect the way individuals resolve issues. Inquiry into moral purposing also is included.

Integrating Field Experiences

Because of the importance of creating a need to know, we propose including field experiences within each learning experience at the beginning of the program instead of incorporating them exclusively at the end of the program. Field experiences create for students a need to know more about a particular issue. At various times during field experiences, students should come together to participate in group activities, converse, problem solve, and dialogue. It would be helpful for participants to bring with them someone from where they are working to strengthen the dialogue and processing of experiences.

At other times in the field experience, students are in schools, gaining a better understanding of the issues. In this manner, students link classroom learning with real problems, resolving real-life issues with their colleagues. Students also can bring their knowledge and skill to the school to assist in tackling important issues. Thus, field experience is integrated throughout the preparation and not only at the end, as is typically the case. Field experiences should be designed to find out what someone needs and wants to know instead of simply to practice what has been learned.

Discovering Meaning Through New Approaches

Whether a leadership development program looks like the one just described or takes a different approach, it is crucial to point out the importance of the meaningfulness and connectedness of the learning experience. Traditional educational administration courses provide students with concepts and content in a systematic fashion dictated by the logic of the subject matter. This puts the cart before the horse as learning does not necessarily proceed in such an orderly manner. In fact, structure and meaning follow experience, and they are discovered by students.

Students must interact with subject matter and discover personal meaning in it (Combs, 1974). The professor's task is to help students to find meaning with the information they acquire. It is only as the meaning of information is perceived that the information becomes useful in advancing human understanding. The discovery of meaning is a personal process involving individual purposes, values, goals, concepts, and needs (Combs, 1974). It is for these reasons that problem-based learning, integrated field experiences, and the manner in which professors organize the learning experience are so important. Ongoing field experiences allow learning experiences to be connected and integrated with one another as well as with the world of practice.

In this chapter we have tried to illustrate the need for change in the entire culture of higher education. Leadership preparation programs must evolve toward a person-centered perspective. This change will require reconceptualizing traditional notions about curriculum and instruction and questioning long-held assumptions about teaching and learning.

We cannot overemphasize the importance of modeling by university faculty members. They truly must accept and demonstrate the beliefs and assumptions we have described throughout this book. In person-centered programs, faculty members treat students as able, worthy, and acceptable, as people of dignity and integrity. Effective university instructors create a learning atmosphere that facilitates each student's self-discovery. They model facilitation and authentic listening skills. They also accept the responsibility to be available to students, and they recognize that interpersonal involvement with students is a top priority.

In these kind of programs, faculty members provide experiences that facilitate making choices and taking personal responsibility in the learning process. They recognize the uniqueness of individual students and value their prior experiences, thus illustrating and acknowledging the principles of adult development. Team teaching and group learning activities demonstrate the importance of collaboration, teamwork, and collegiality. Faculty members also model the importance of developing linkages with K–12 education by seeking out creative ways for graduate students to become involved in schools.

Leadership preparation programs can become places where instructors encourage and assist the processes of learning and the discovery of meaning. They can become places where graduate students are immersed in rich and purposeful experiences. But these kinds of programs will not emerge without massive changes in the beliefs and attitudes of many professors. That task is enormous, but it is desperately needed if person-centered leadership is to become a reality.

BIBLIOGRAPHY

Argyris, C., & Schon, D. (1975). *Theory in practice: Increasing professional effectiveness*. San Francisco: Jossey-Bass.

Astuto, T., Clark, D., Read, A., McGree, K., & Fernandez, L. (1994). *Roots of reform: Challenging assumptions that control education reform*. Bloomington, IN: Phi Delta Kappa.

Barnett, B., Caffarella, R., Daresh, J., King, R., Nicholson, T., & Whitaker, K. S. (1992). A new slant on leadership preparation. *Educational Leadership, 49*(5), 72–76.

Barnett, B., & Whitaker, K. S. (1996). *Restructuring for student learning (The school leader's library)*. Lancaster, PA: Technomic Publishing.

Bennett, C. (1993). Teacher researchers: All dressed up and no place to go. *Educational Leadership, 51*(2), 69–70.

Bridges, E. (1992). *Problem based learning for administrators*. Eugene: University of Oregon, ERIC Clearinghouse on Educational Management.

Caine, R. N., & Caine, G. (1991). *Making connections: Teaching and the human brain*. Alexandria, VA: Association for Supervision and Curriculum Development.

Carnegie Council for Adolescent Development. (1989). *Turning points*. Washington, DC: Author.

Combs, A. W. (1962a). A perceptual view of the adequate personality. In A. W. Combs (Ed.), *Perceiving, behaving, becoming: A new focus for education* (1962 ASCD Yearbook, pp. 50–64). Alexandria, VA: Association for Supervision and Curriculum Development.

Combs, A. W. (Ed.). (1962b). *Perceiving, behaving, becoming: A new focus for education*. Alexandria, VA: Association for Supervision and Curriculum Development.

Combs, A. (1974). *The professional education of teachers: A humanistic approach to teacher preparation*. Boston: Allyn & Bacon.

Combs, A. W. (1982). *A personal approach to teaching: Beliefs that make a difference*. Boston: Allyn & Bacon.

Combs, A. W. (1986). What makes a good helper? *Person-Centered Review, 1*, 51–62.

Combs, A. W. (1992). *The schools we need*. Lanham, MD: University Press of America.

Combs, A. W., & Avila, D. (1985). *Helping relationships: Basic concepts for the helping professions*. Boston: Allyn & Bacon.

Combs, A. W., & Gonzalez, D. M. (1997). *Helping relationships: Basic concepts for the helping professions* (4th ed.). Boston: Allyn & Bacon.

Combs, A. W., & Soper, D. W. (1963). The perceptual organization of effective counselors. *Journal of Counseling Psychology, 10*, 222–227.

Elena, W. J., Stevenson, M., & Webb, H. V. (1961). *Who's a good teacher?* Washington, DC: American Association of School Administrators.

The Holmes Group. (1986). *Tomorrow's teachers*. East Lansing, MI: Author.

Kohn, A. (1994). The truth about self-esteem. *Phi Delta Kappan, 4*, 272–283.

Little, J. W. (1982). Norms of collegiality and experimentation: Workplace conditions of school success. *American Educational Research Journal, 3*, 325–340.

Maslow, A. H. (1954). *Motivation and personality*. New York: Harper & Brothers.

Mirel, J. (1994). School reform unplugged: The Bensenville New American School project, 1991–1993. *American Educational Research Journal, 3*, 481–518.

Miser, A. B. (1995). Moral dilemmas of the school principalship. (Doctoral dissertation, University of Northern Colorado, 1995). *Dissertation Abstracts International, A 56/08*, 2958.

Murphy, J. (1992). *The landscape of leadership preparation: Reframing the education of school administrators*. Newbury Park, CA: Corwin Press.

Murphy, J. (1993). Restructuring: In search of a movement. In J. Murphy & P. Hallinger (Eds.), *Restructuring schooling: Learning from ongoing efforts* (pp. 1–31). Newbury Park, CA: Corwin Press.

National Commission on Excellence in Education Administration. (1987). *Leaders for America's schools.* Tempe, AZ: University Council for Educational Administration.

Osterman, K., & Kottkamp, R. (1993). *Reflective practice for educators: Improving schooling through professional development.* Newbury Park, CA: Corwin Press.

Peterson, K. D. (1981, April). *Making sense of principals' work.* Paper presented at the annual meeting of the American Educational Research Association, Los Angeles.

Purkey, W. (1970). *Self-concept and student achievement.* Englewood Cliffs, NJ: Prentice Hall.

Roberts, L. (1990). *Reinventing school leadership.* (Working memo prepared for the Reinventing School Leadership Conference). Cambridge, MA: National Center for Educational Leadership.

Rogers, C. (1962). Toward becoming a fully functioning person. In A. W. Combs (Ed.), *Perceiving, behaving, becoming: A new focus for education* (pp. 21–33). Alexandria, VA: Association for Supervision and Curriculum Development.

Sadker, M., & Sadker, D. (1994). *Failing at fairness.* New York: Touchstone.

Senge, P. M. (1990). *The fifth discipline: The art and practice of the learning organization.* New York: Doubleday.

Sergiovanni, T. (1994). *Building community in schools.* San Francisco: Jossey-Bass.

Sergiovanni, T., & Starratt, R. (1979). *Supervision: Human perspectives.* New York: McGraw-Hill.

Shore, R. (1995). How one high school improved school climate. *Educational Leadership, 52*(5), 76–78.

Wheatley, M. J. (1992). *Leadership and the new science: Learning about organization from an orderly universe.* San Francisco: Berrett-Koehler.

Wheatley, M. J., & Kellner-Rogers, M. (1996). *A simpler way.* San Francisco: Berrett-Koehler.

Whitaker, K. S. (1996). Exploring causes of principal burnout. *Journal of Educational Administration, 34*(1), 60–71.

INDEX

ABOUT THE AUTHORS

Arthur W. Combs is a noted teacher, consultant, and psychologist. In 1947, along with Donald Snygg, he invented perceptual-experiential psychology, a systematic frame of reference for the study of persons. He is past president of the Association for Supervision and Curriculum Development and served as the editor of the 1962 ASCD Yearbook, *Perceiving, Behaving, Becoming*. He has written 22 books and monographs and more than 150 articles on psychology, counseling, and education.

Ann B. Miser has held the positions of high school teacher, assistant principal, associate principal, and principal. She served as a high school principal in Vermont and as the secondary principal of the University of Northern Colorado Laboratory School in Greeley, Colorado. Currently, she teaches in the School of Education at Colorado State University and coordinates a Professional Development School site at a high school in Fort Collins, Colorado.

Kathryn S. Whitaker also is experienced in K–12 and higher education. She has held positions as a middle school teacher, high school assistant principal, and elementary principal. She is coauthor, with Bruce Barnett, of a 1996 book, *Restructuring for Student Learning*

(*A School Leader's Library*). Currently, she teaches in the Division of Educational Leadership and Policy Studies at the University of Northern Colorado, a position she has held for 10 years. During the 1996–97 school year, she participated in a job exchange with an elementary principal so she could renew her leadership skills in an elementary setting.

Contact the authors at the following addresses:

Arthur W. Combs
1975 28th Ave.
Greeley, CO 80631
E-mail: artcombs@info2000.net

Ann B. Miser
School of Education
Colorado State University
Fort Collins, CO 80523-1588
Phone: 970-491-1172
Fax: 970-491-1317
E-mail: miser@CAHS.Colostate.edu

Kathryn S. Whitaker
College of Education
University of Northern Colorado
Greeley, CO 80639
Phone: 970-351-2507
Fax: 970-351-3334
E-mail: whitaker@edtech.unco.edu